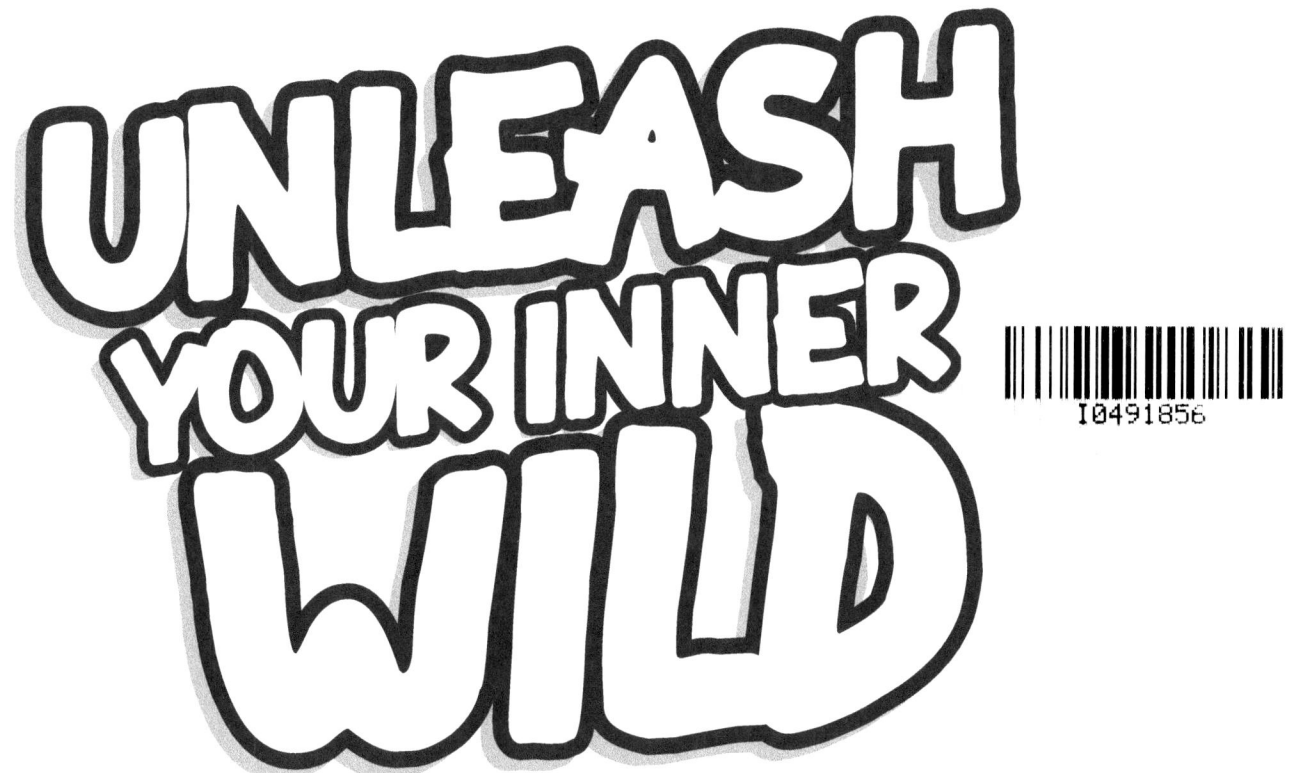

UNLEASH YOUR INNER WILD

Irreverent & inspirational
stress relieving
coloring book f
or adults

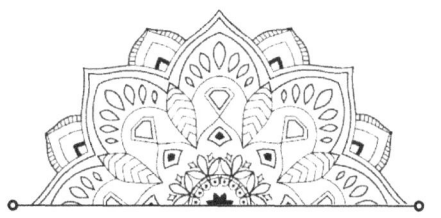

Emma Russo

Introduction

Connect with yourself and enjoy pure animal wisdom.

Have you realized that animals are the best Mindfulness teachers? They don't live wondering if they paid the bills or if their partner called, they live in the present and surrender to the wonders of life.

Ready? The good stuff is about to begin! My name is Emma Russo and my passion is creative Mindfulness to unwind yourself from everything, and bringing it to everyone with a little spark, fun and irreverence is my mission in this book.

I truly congratulate you for embracing the art of Mindfulness along with the wildest animals. Mindfulness is an art used for many years to reduce levels of stress, anxiety, insomnia and invites us to wonderful states of relaxation for those who practice it. It is never too late to start practicing, unless you are a bottle of wine or a good cheese, age does not matter!

It is time to relax in your favorite place, leaving everything and everyone aside. This just begins! With this book you will be able to calm your emotions as if calming a wild colt, or maybe.... you will unleash the wild colt that you have inside!

I wish you every success in this new adventure.

Emma R.

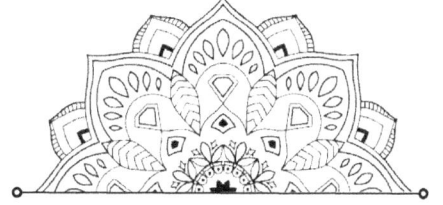

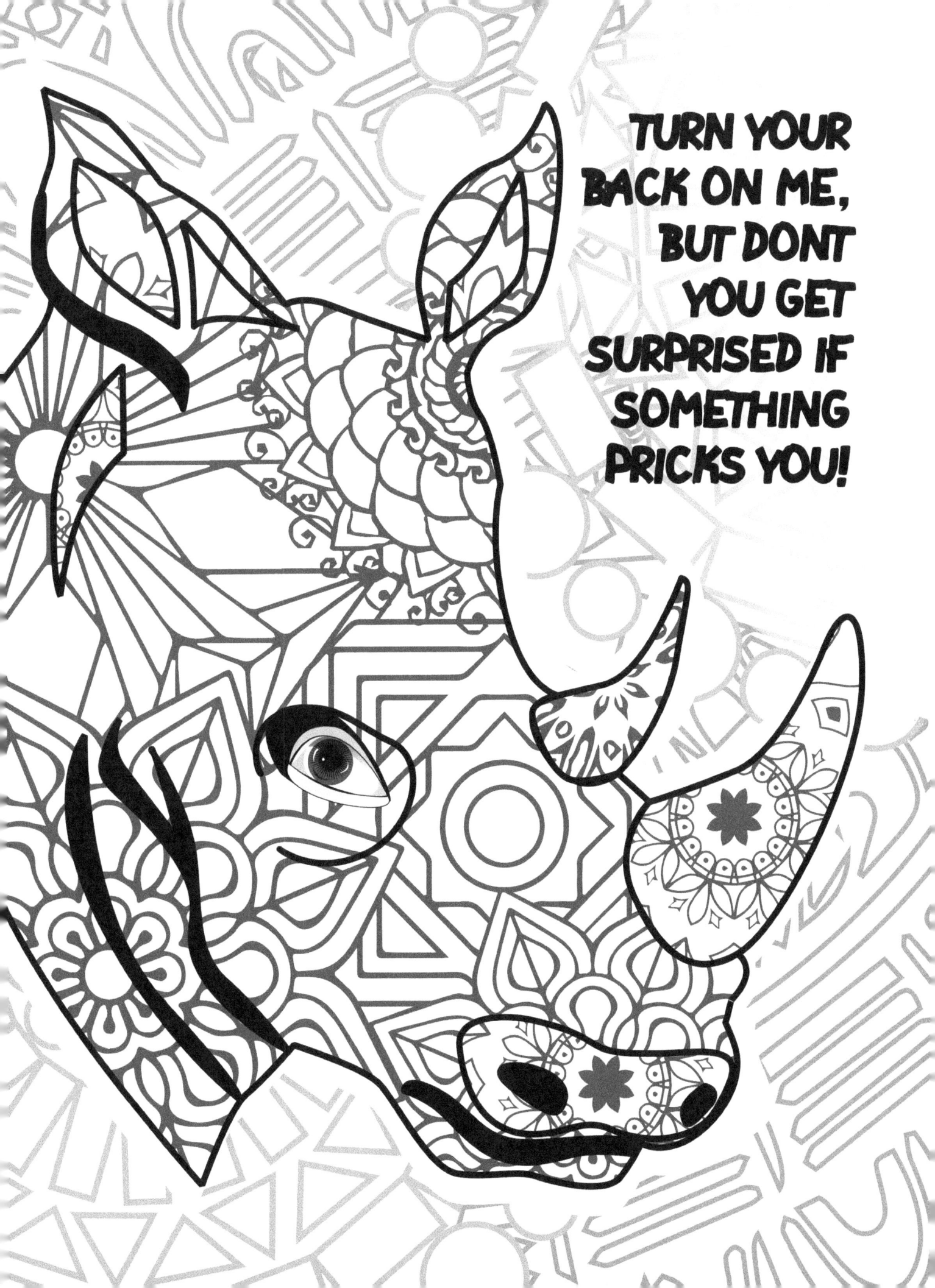

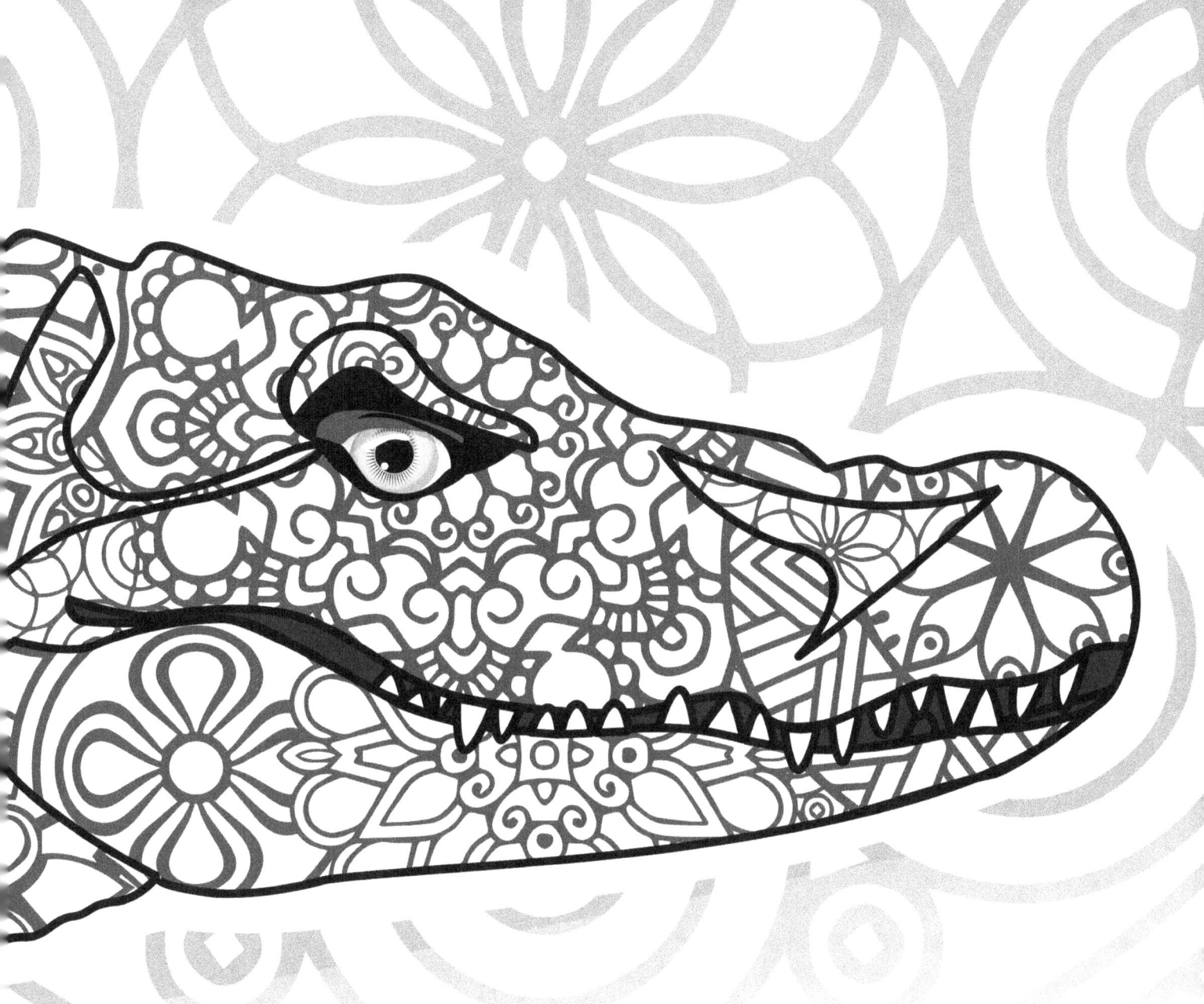

HELL I WILL BITE YOU
IF I GET HUNGRY

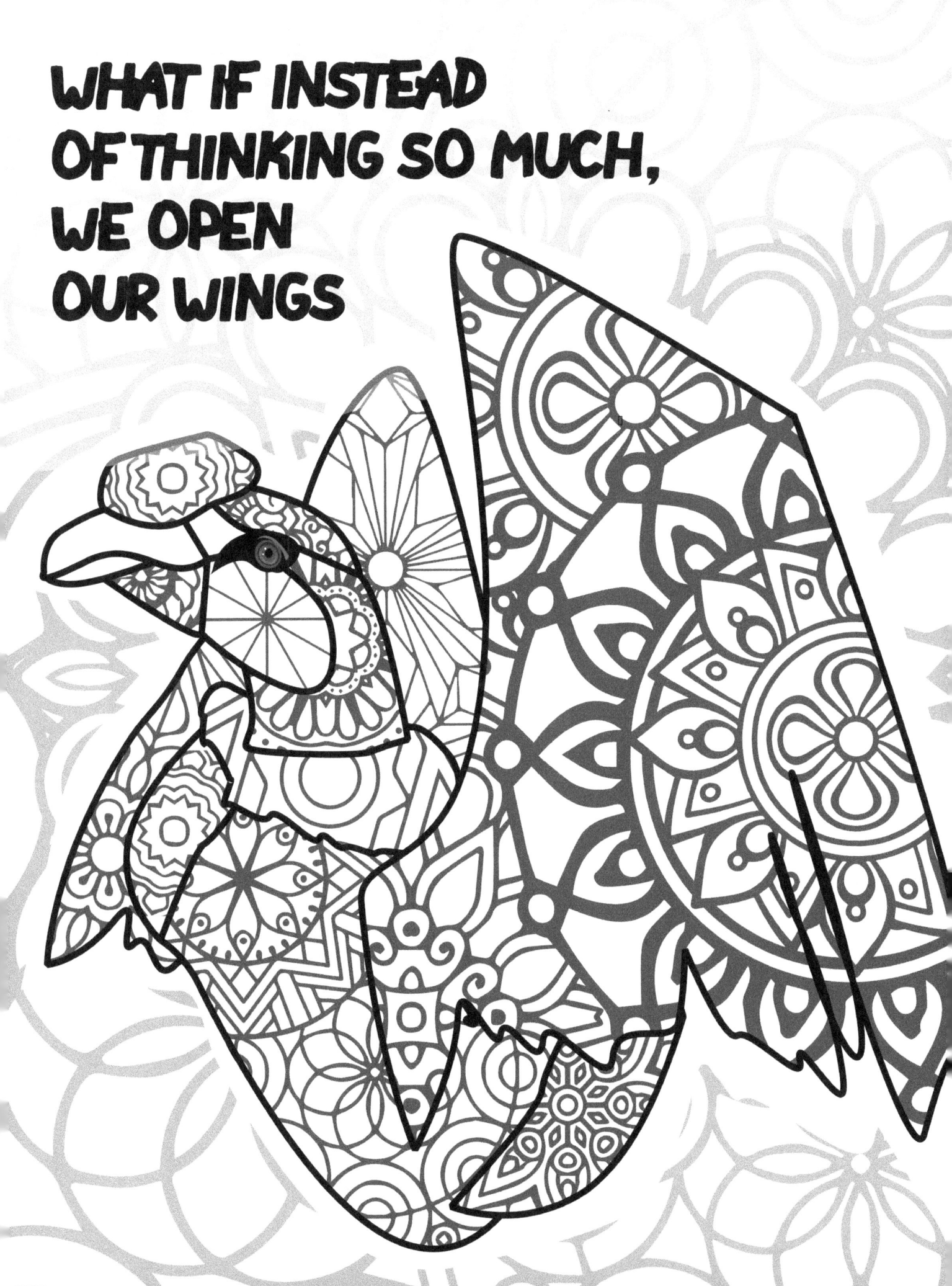

WHAT IF INSTEAD
OF THINKING SO MUCH,
WE OPEN
OUR WINGS

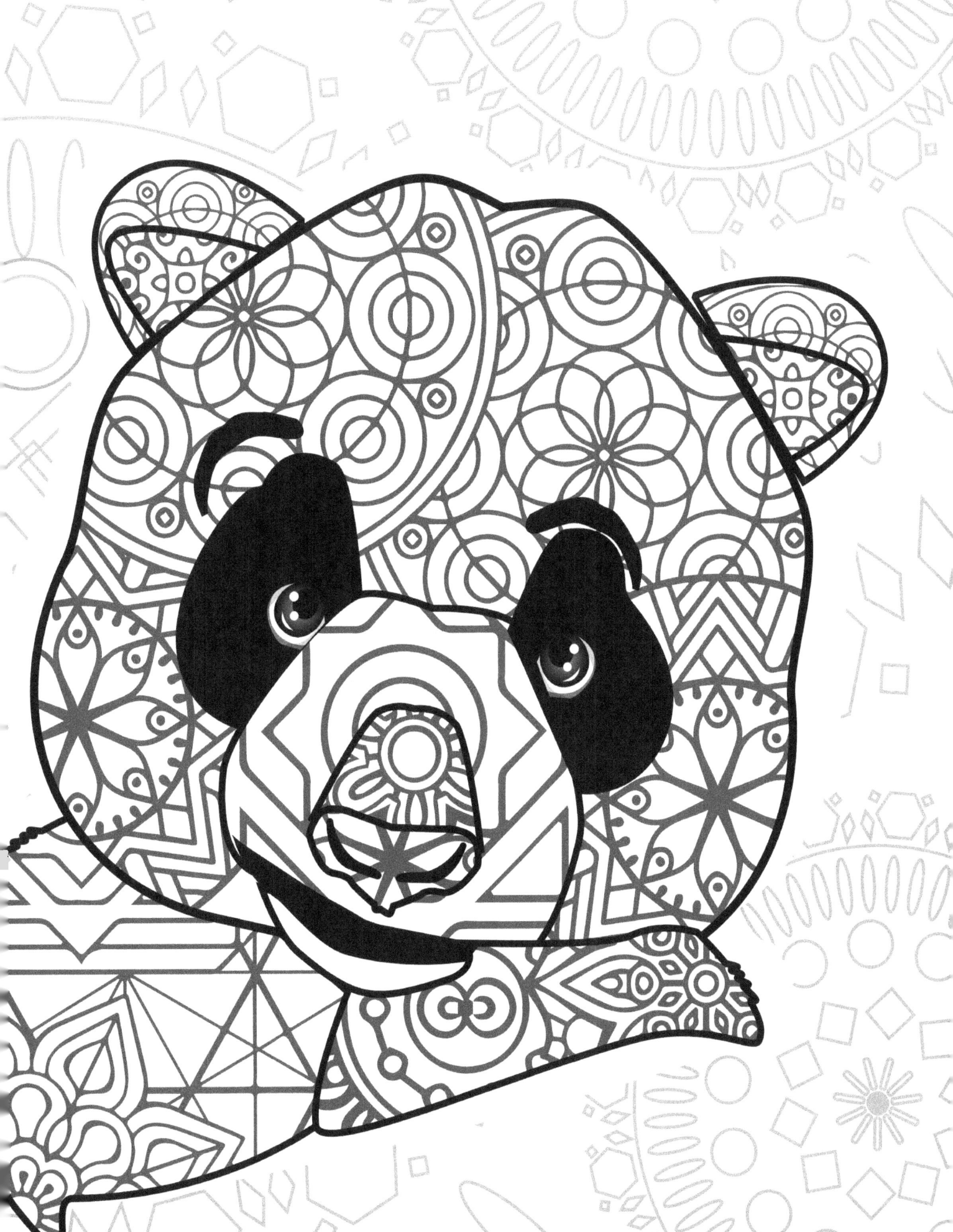

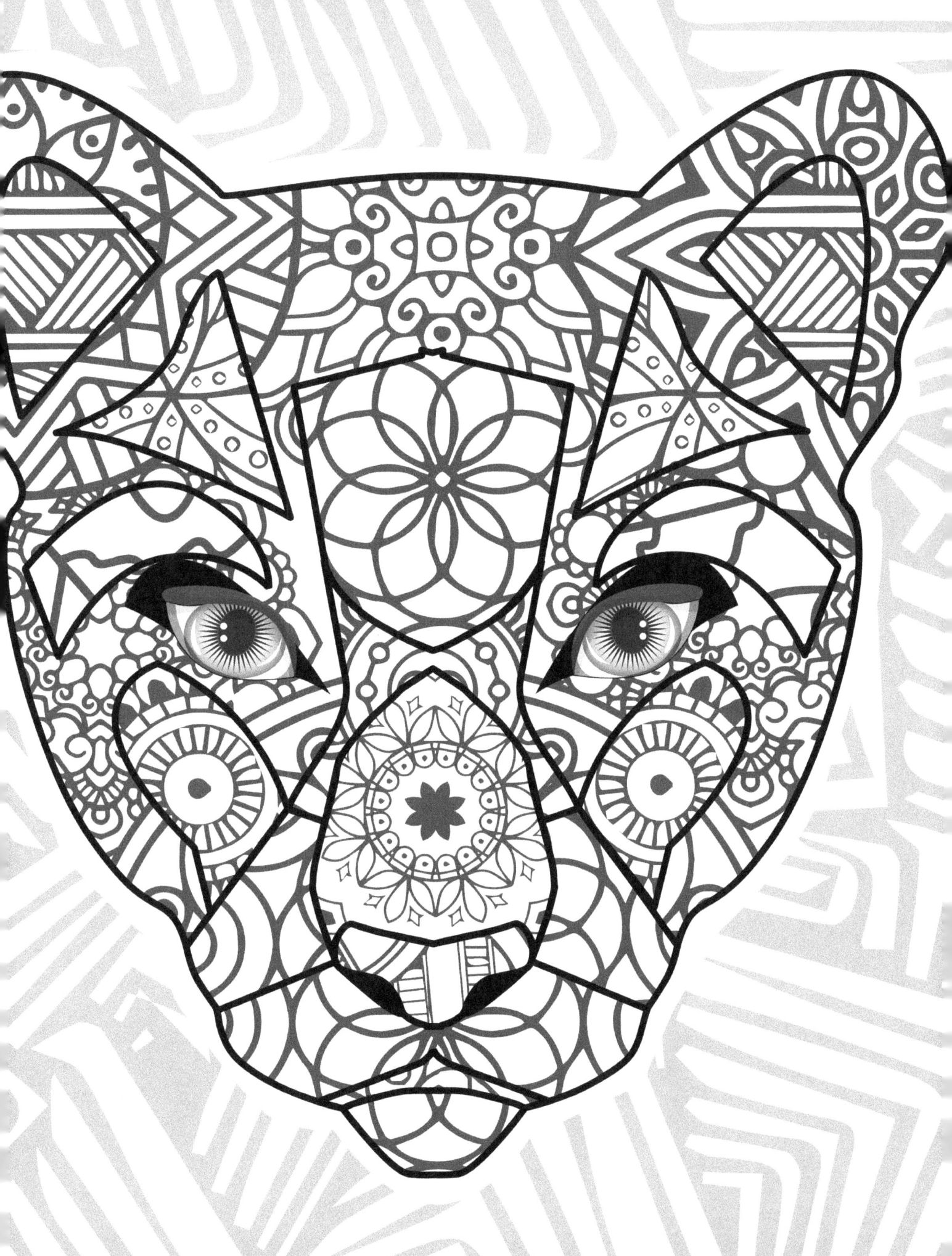

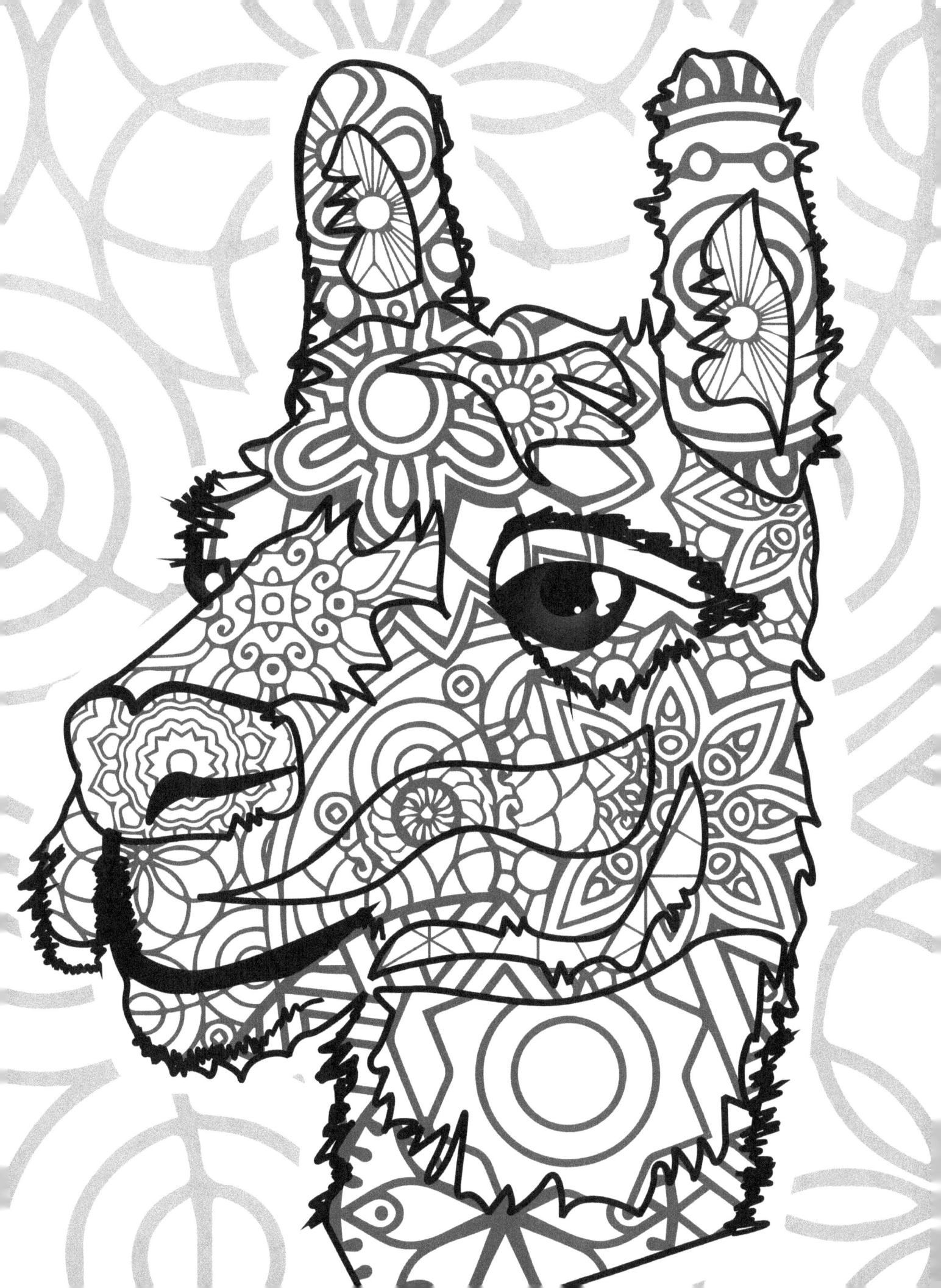

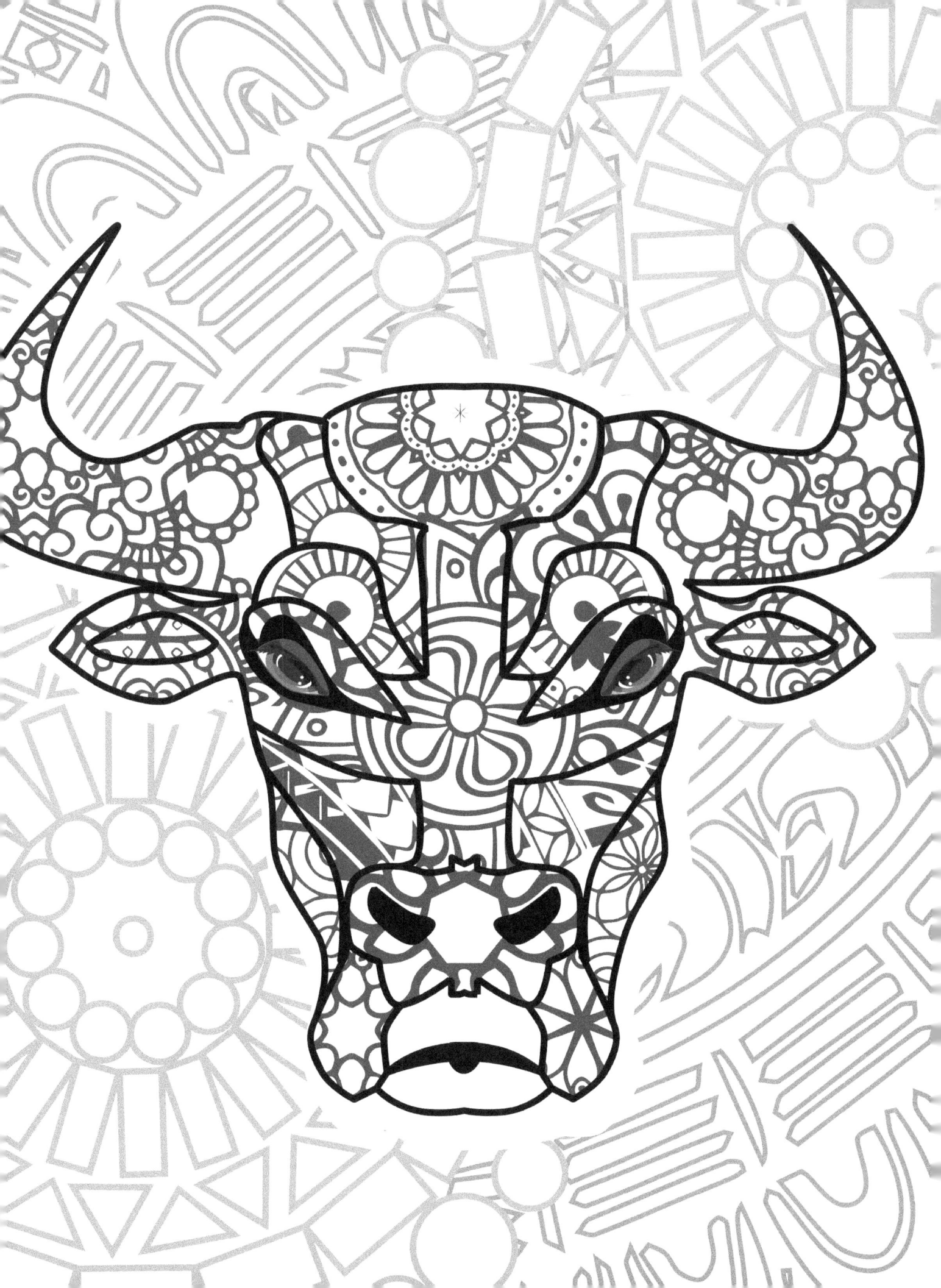

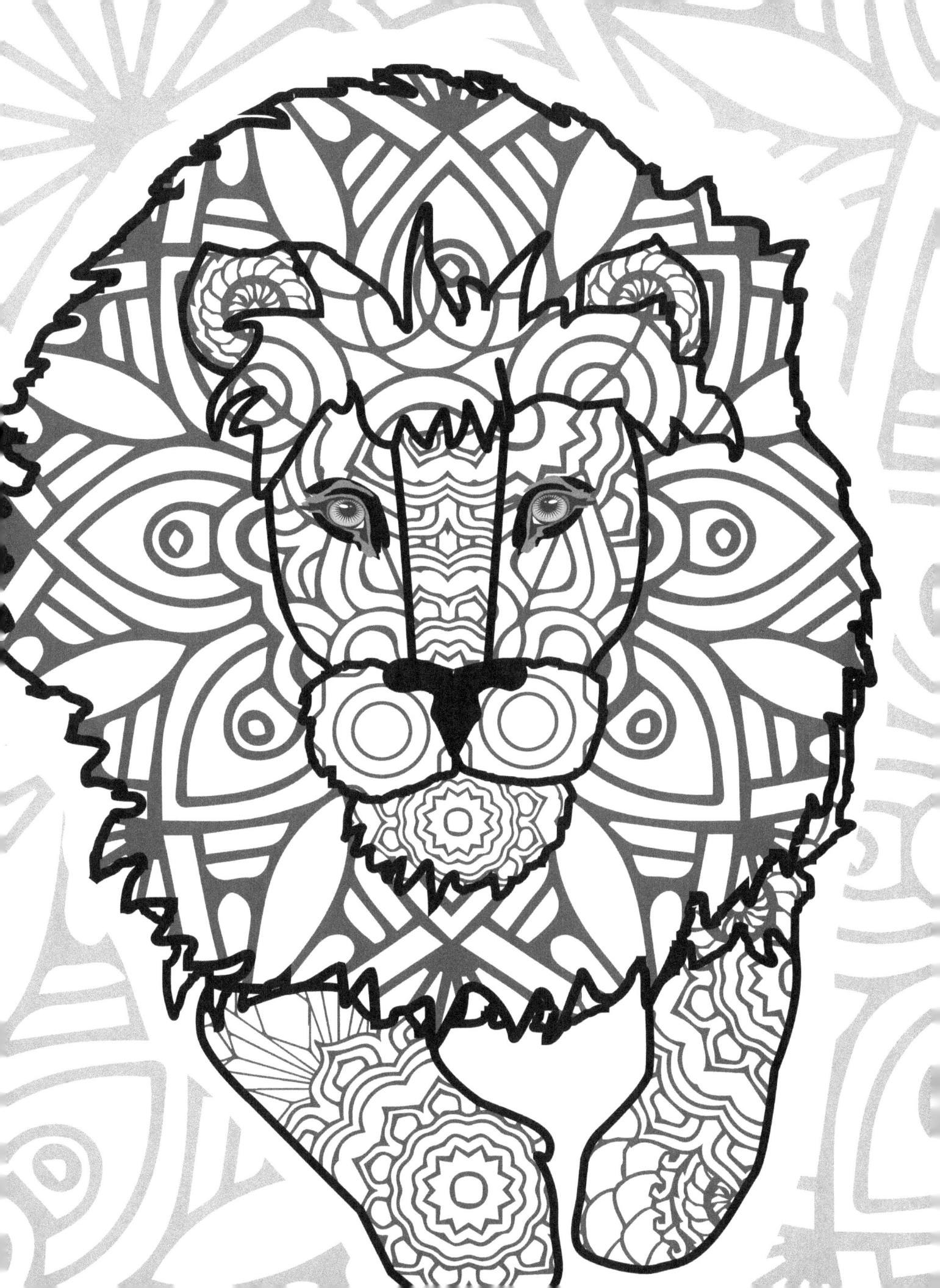

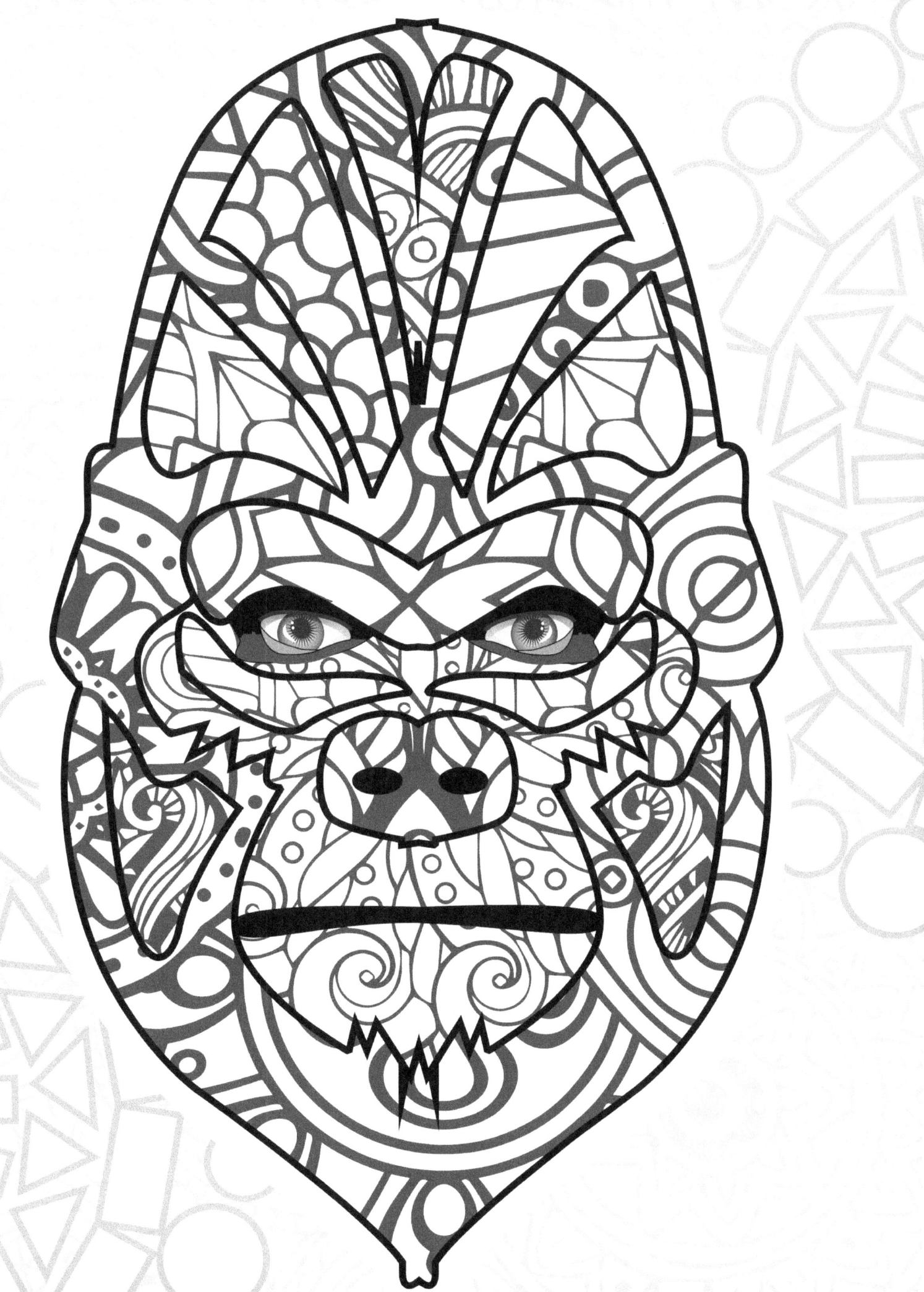

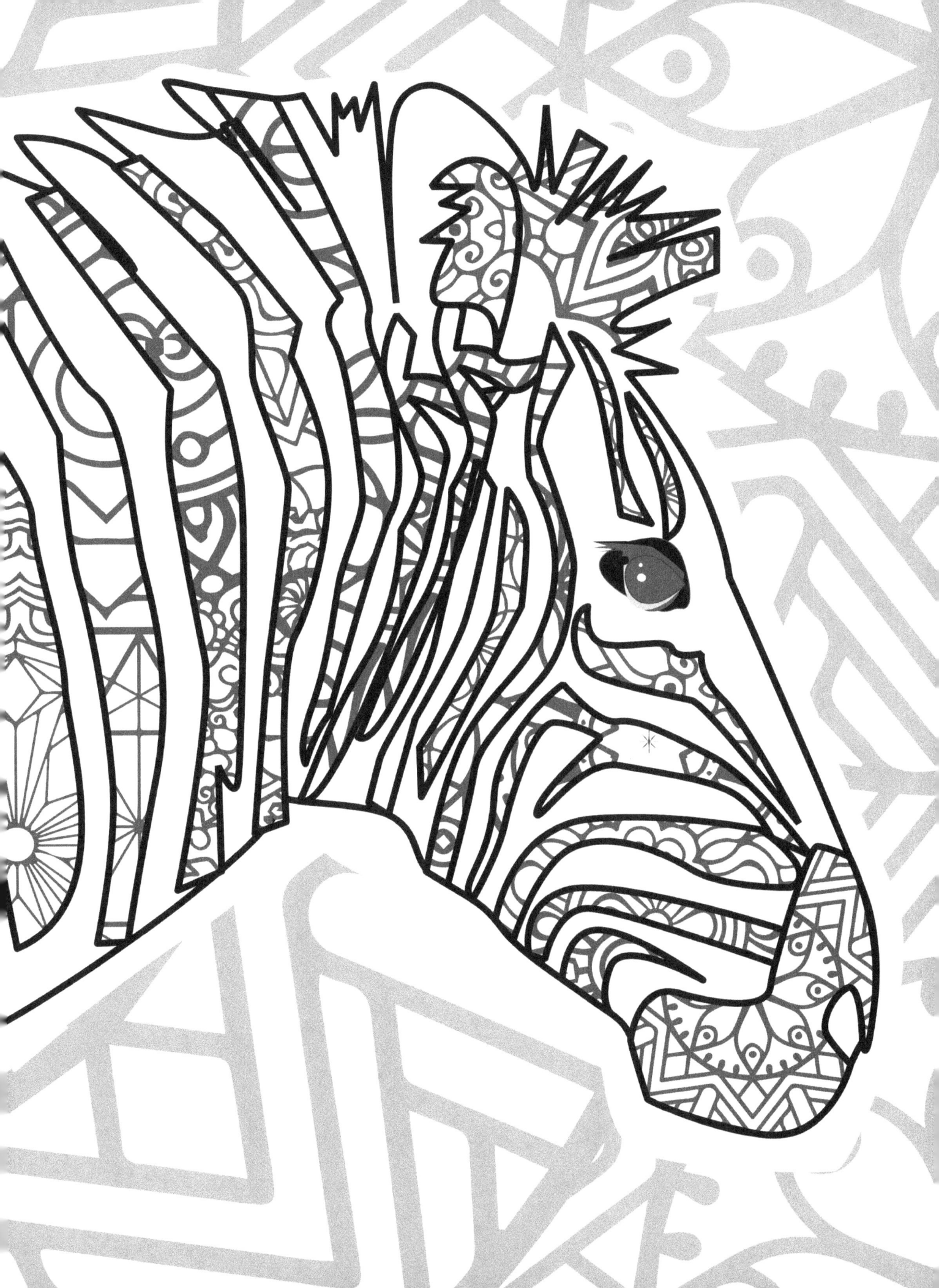

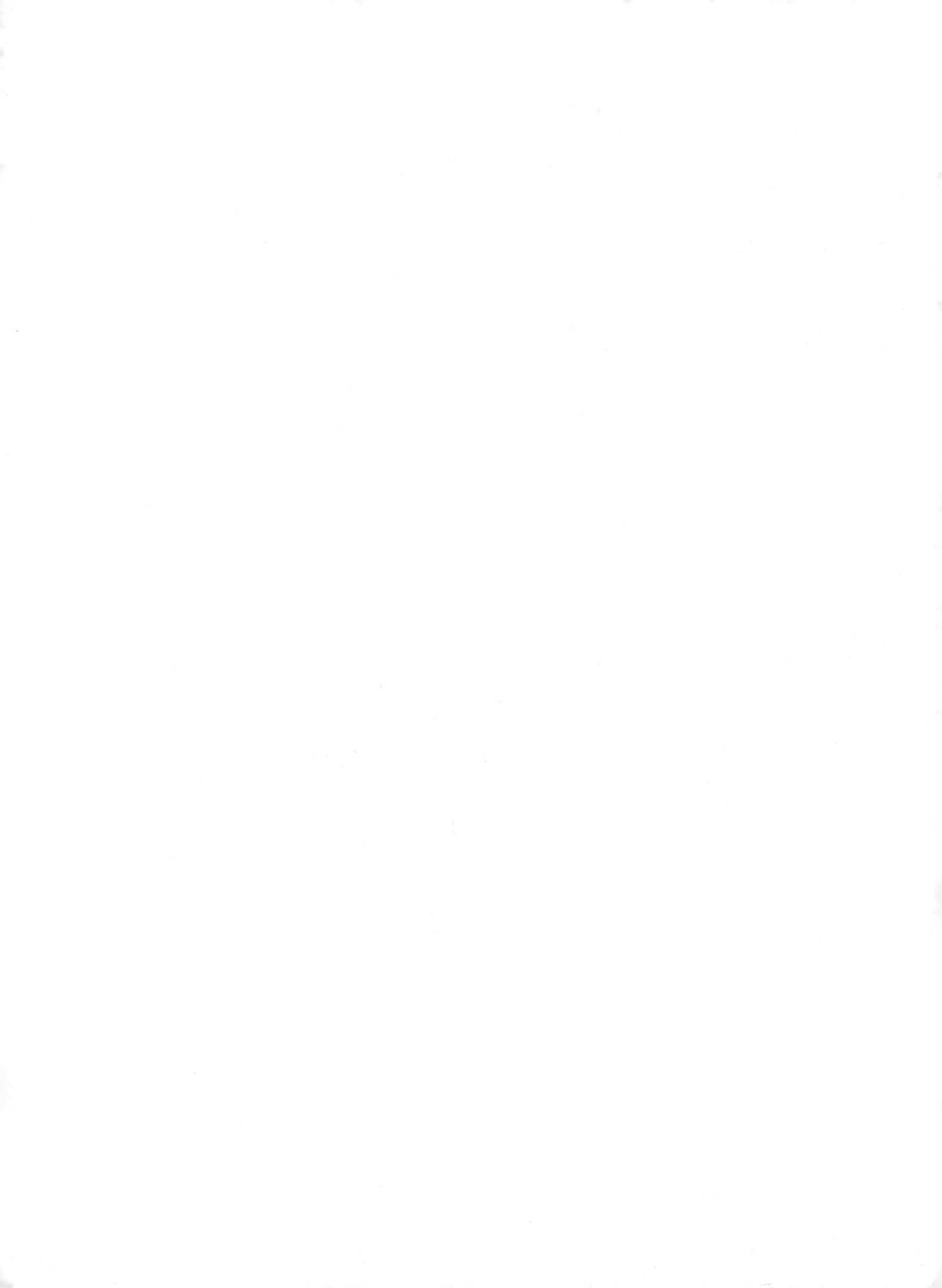

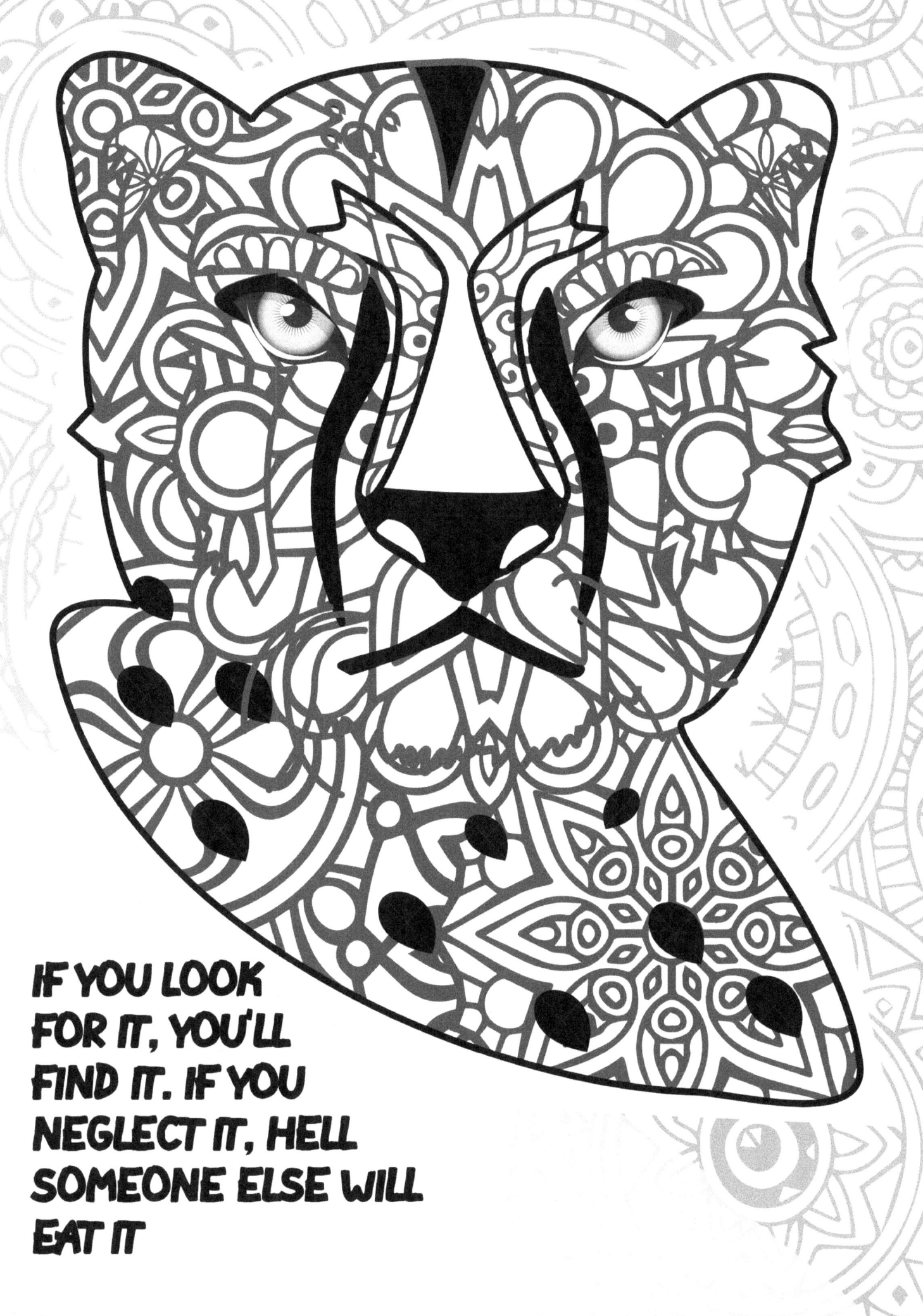

IF YOU LOOK FOR IT, YOU'LL FIND IT. IF YOU NEGLECT IT, HELL SOMEONE ELSE WILL EAT IT

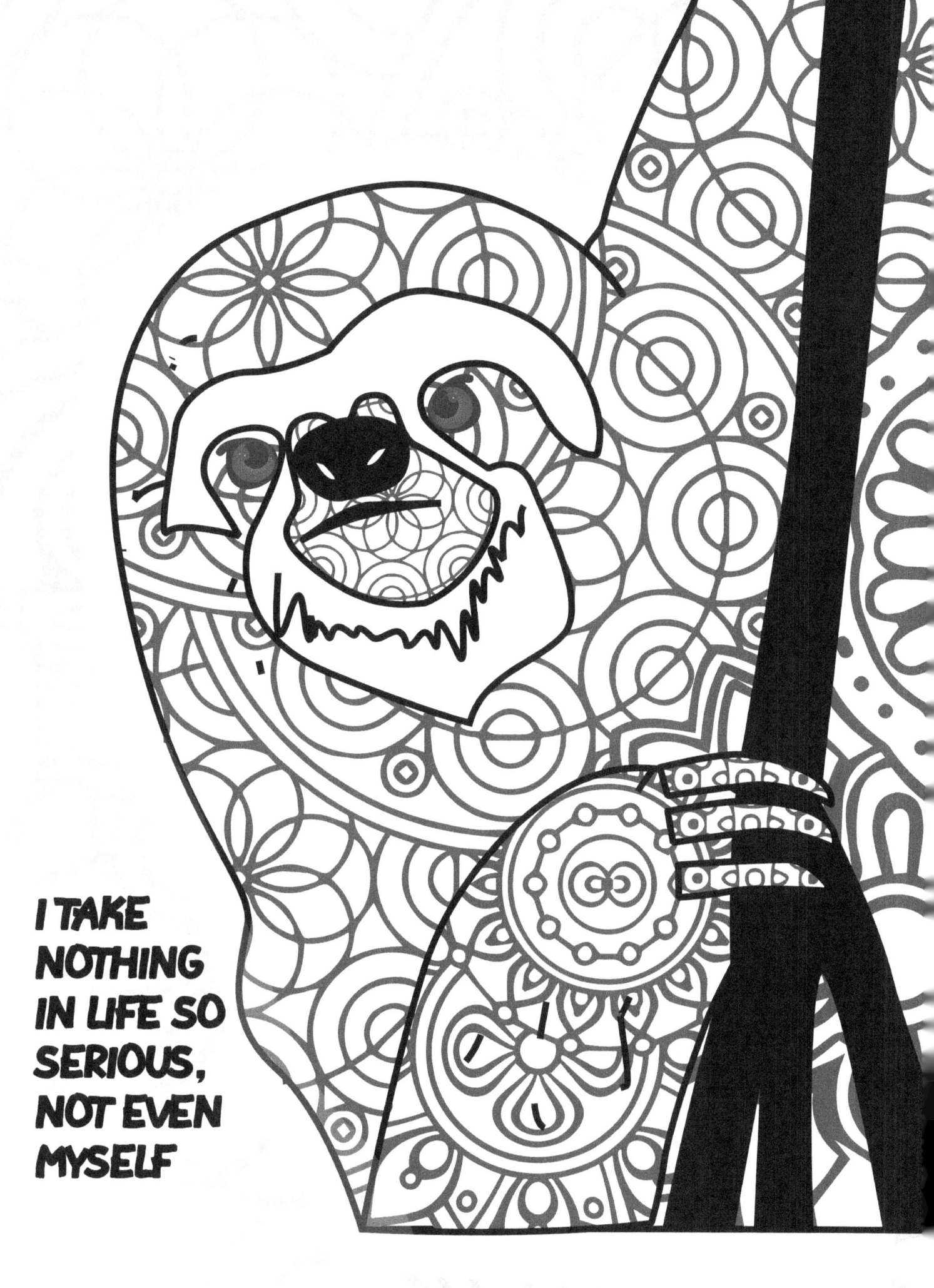

I TAKE
NOTHING
IN LIFE SO
SERIOUS,
NOT EVEN
MYSELF

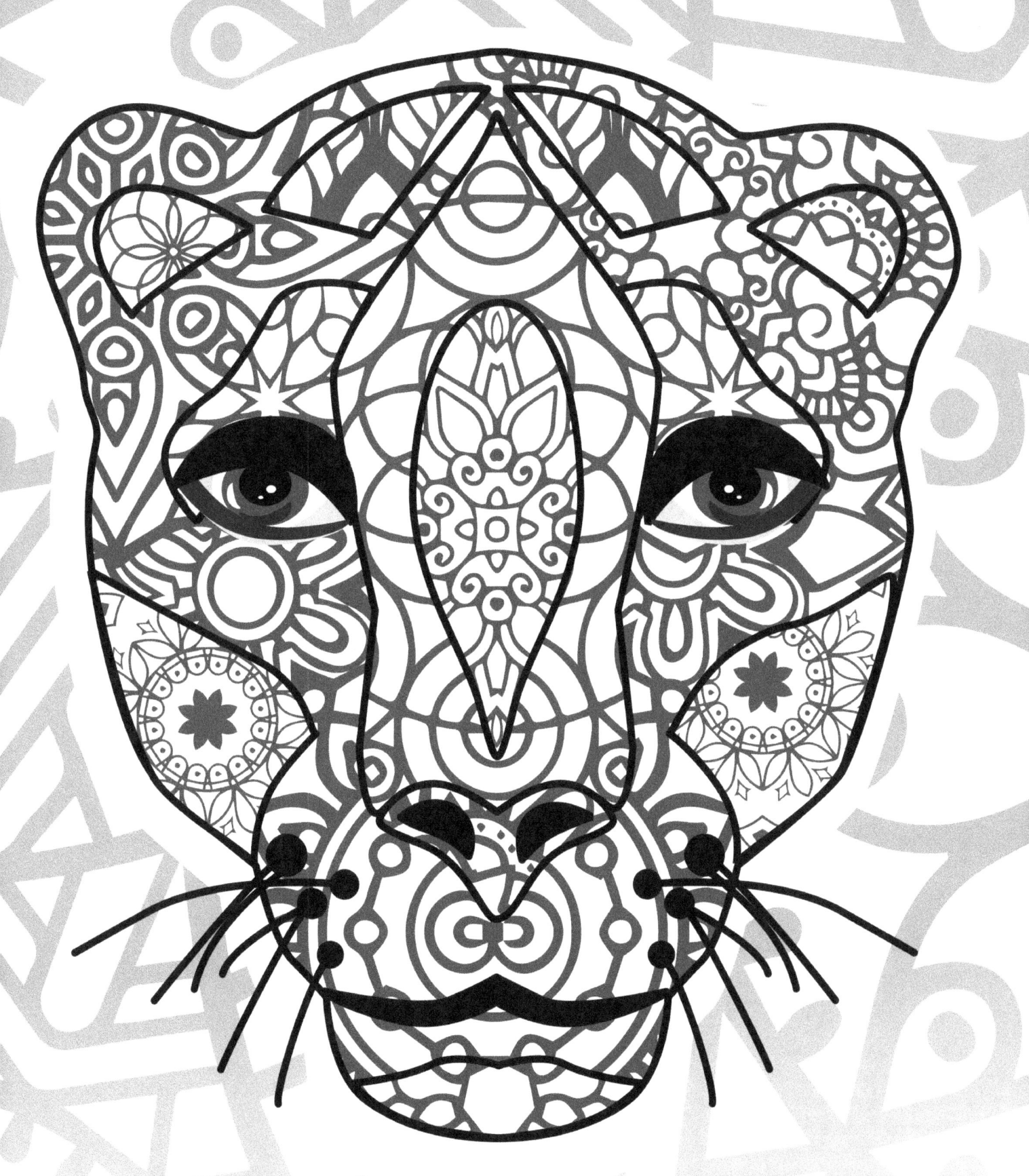

DON'T FORBID IT BECAUSE
I'LL WANT IT EVEN MORE

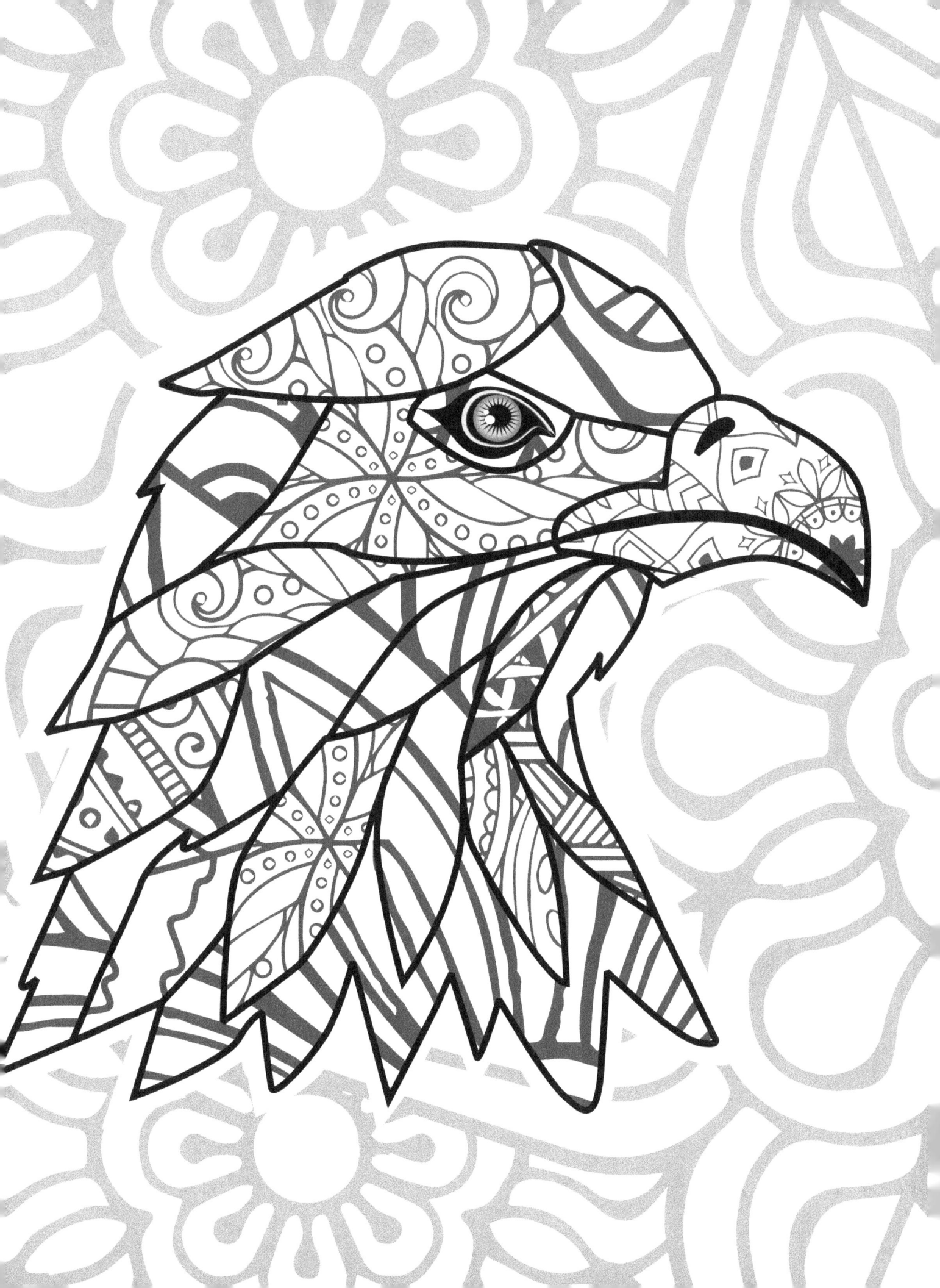

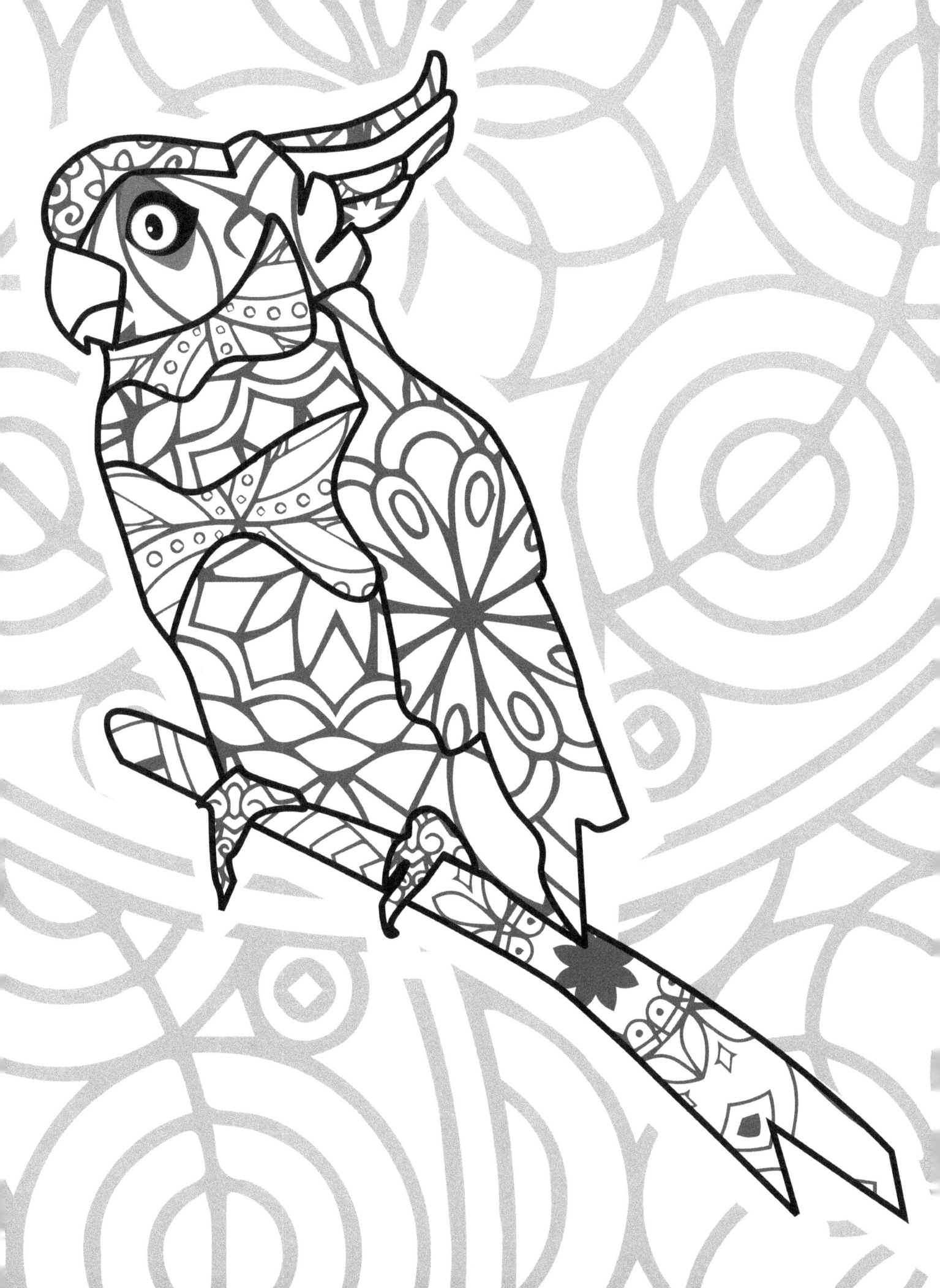

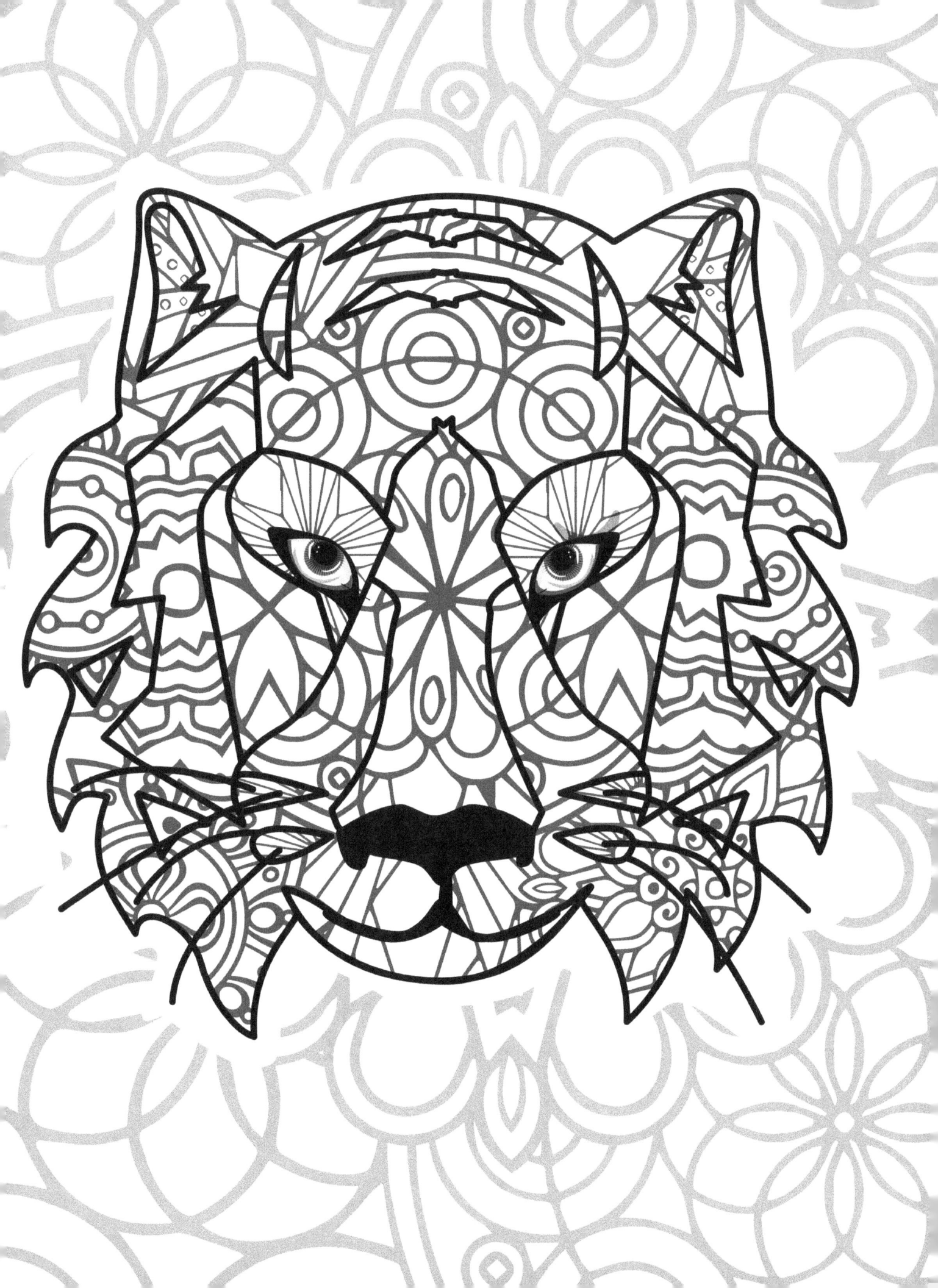

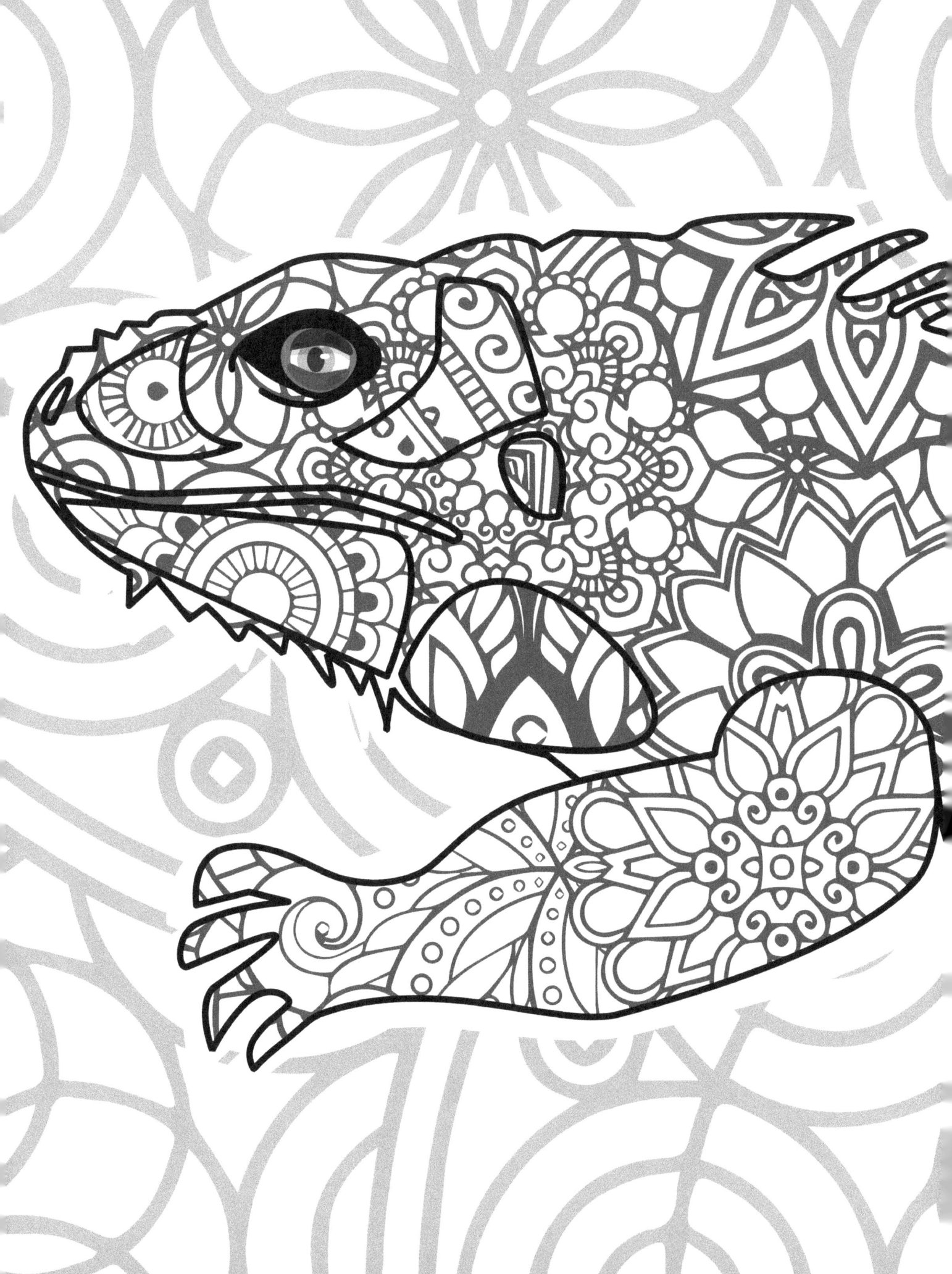

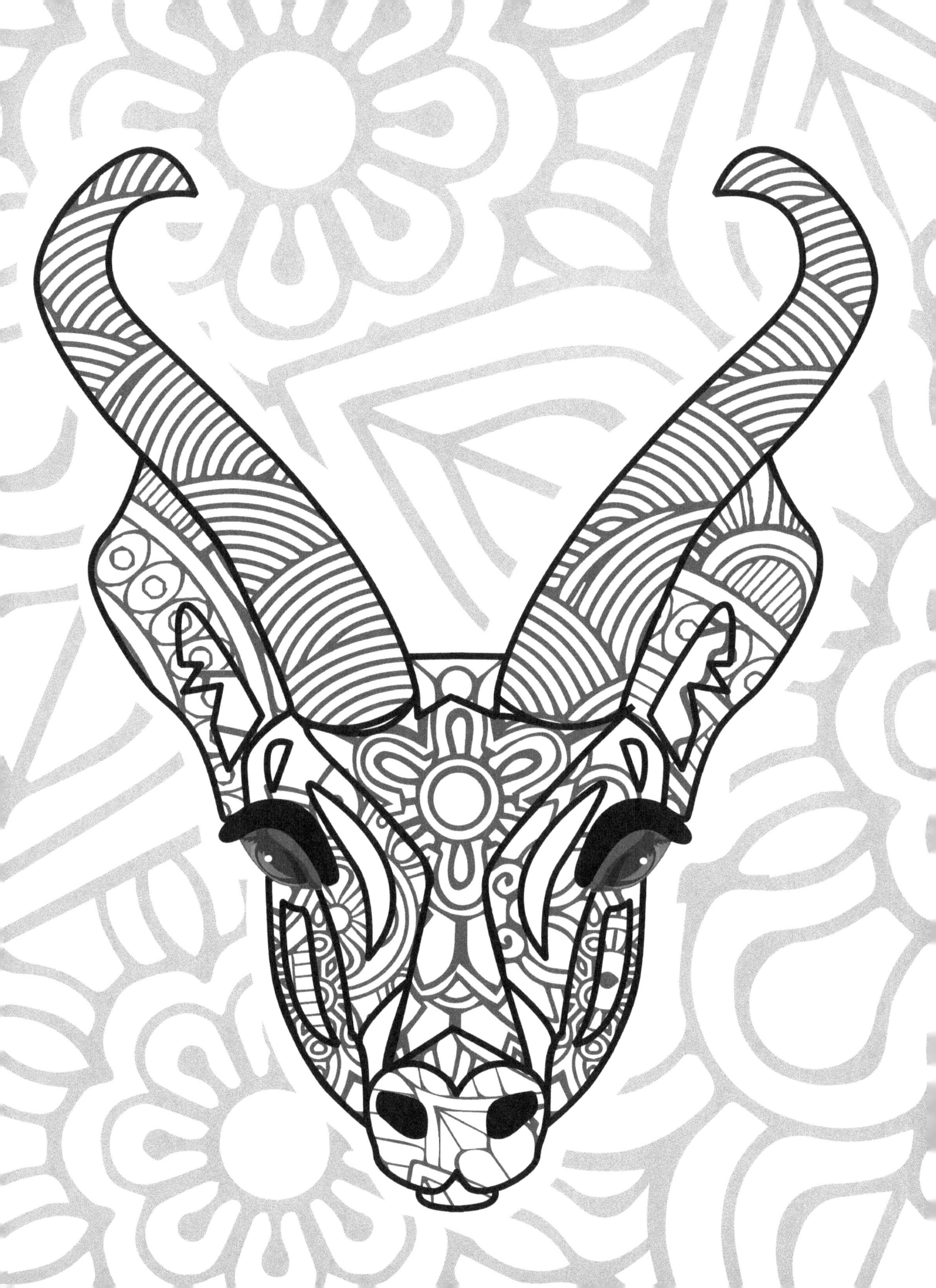

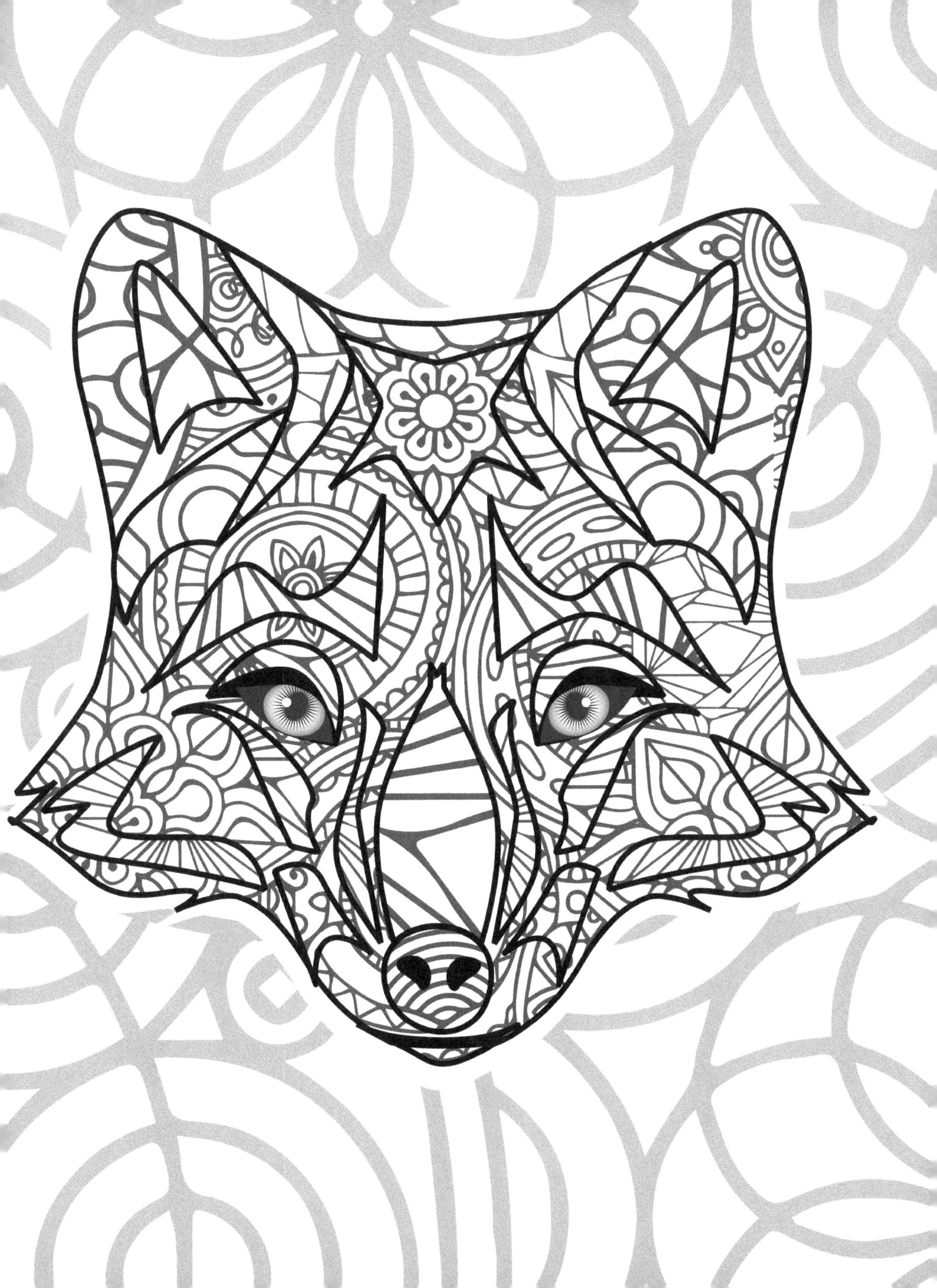

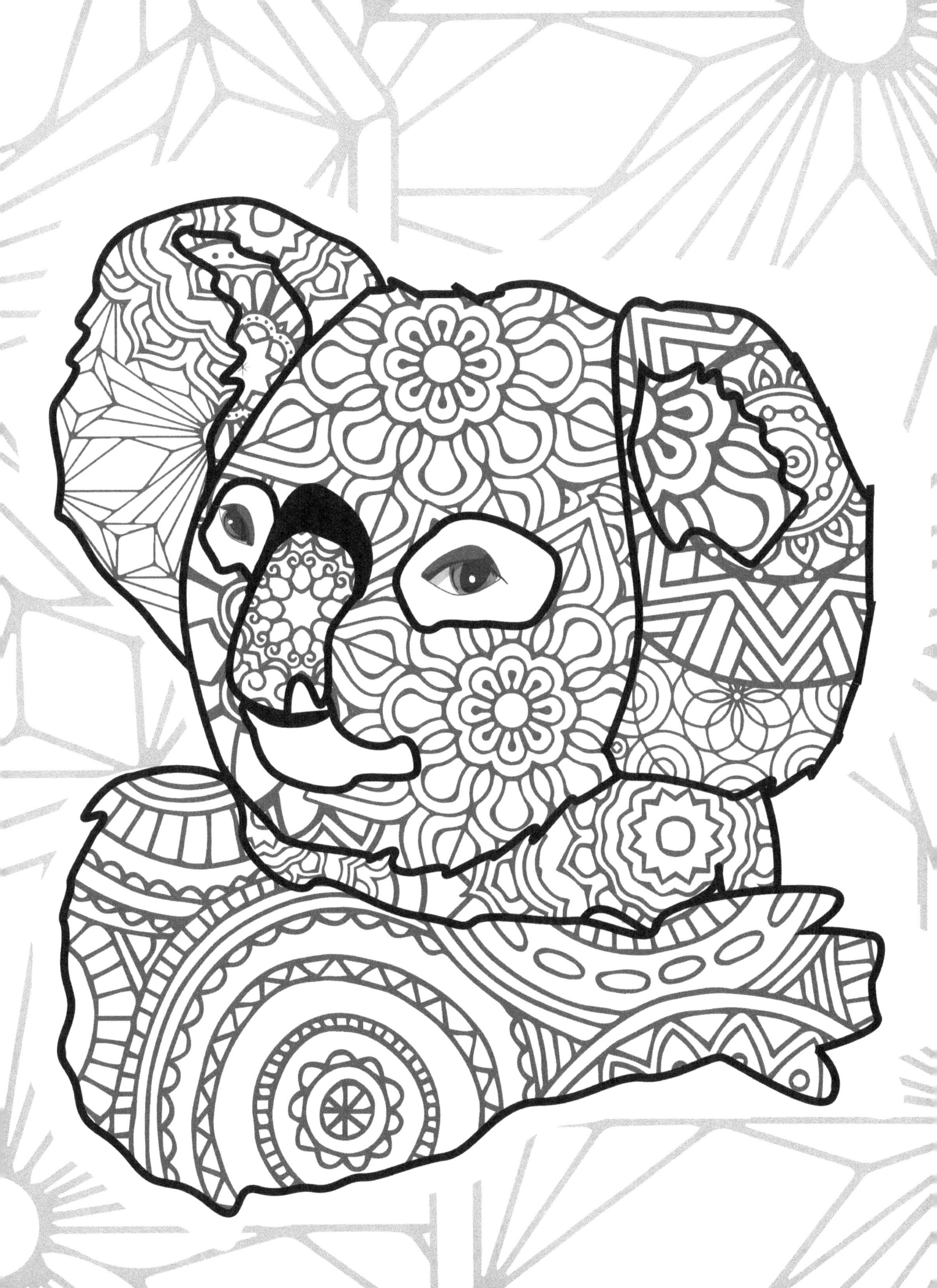

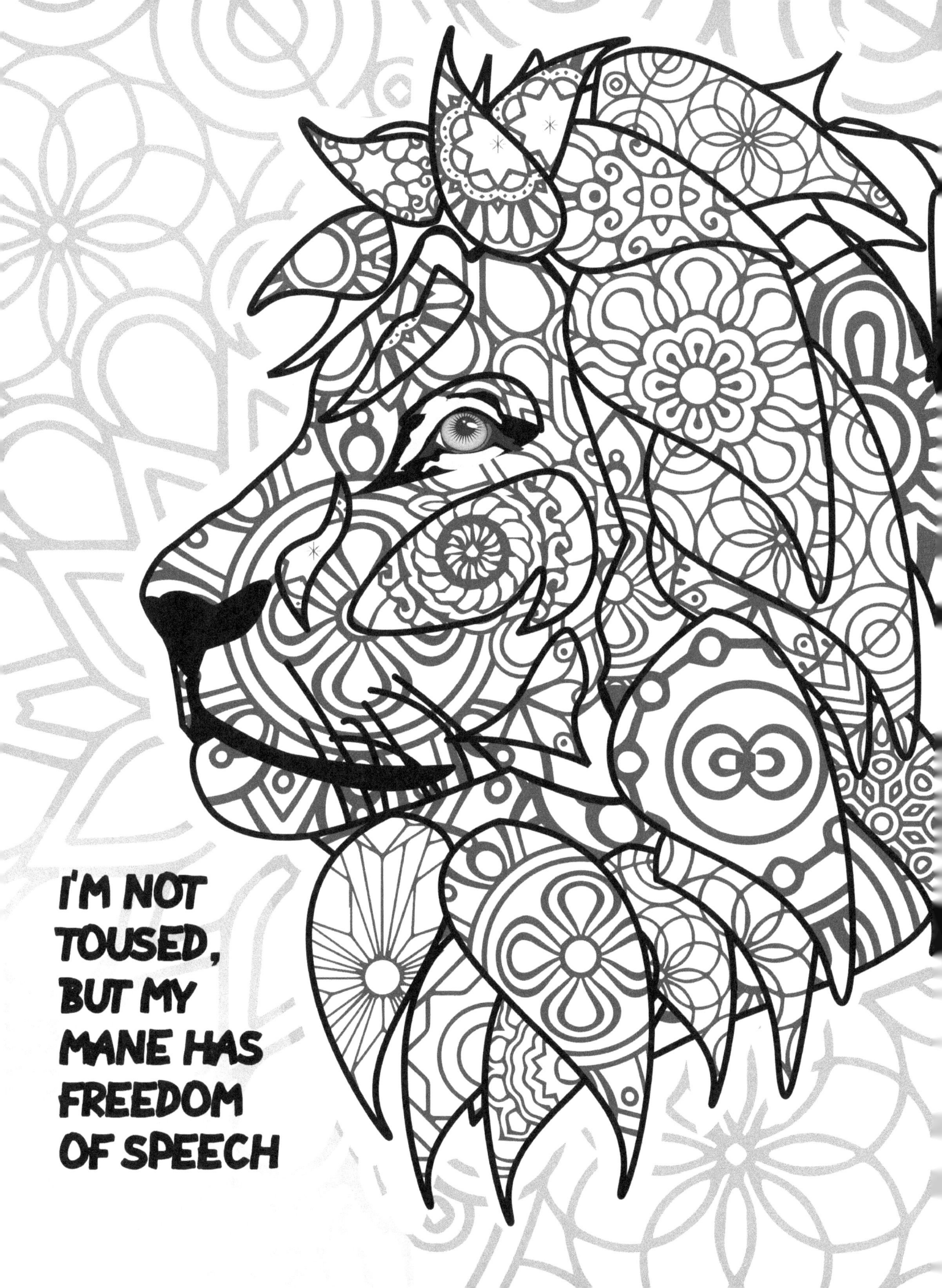

I'M NOT
TOUSED,
BUT MY
MANE HAS
FREEDOM
OF SPEECH

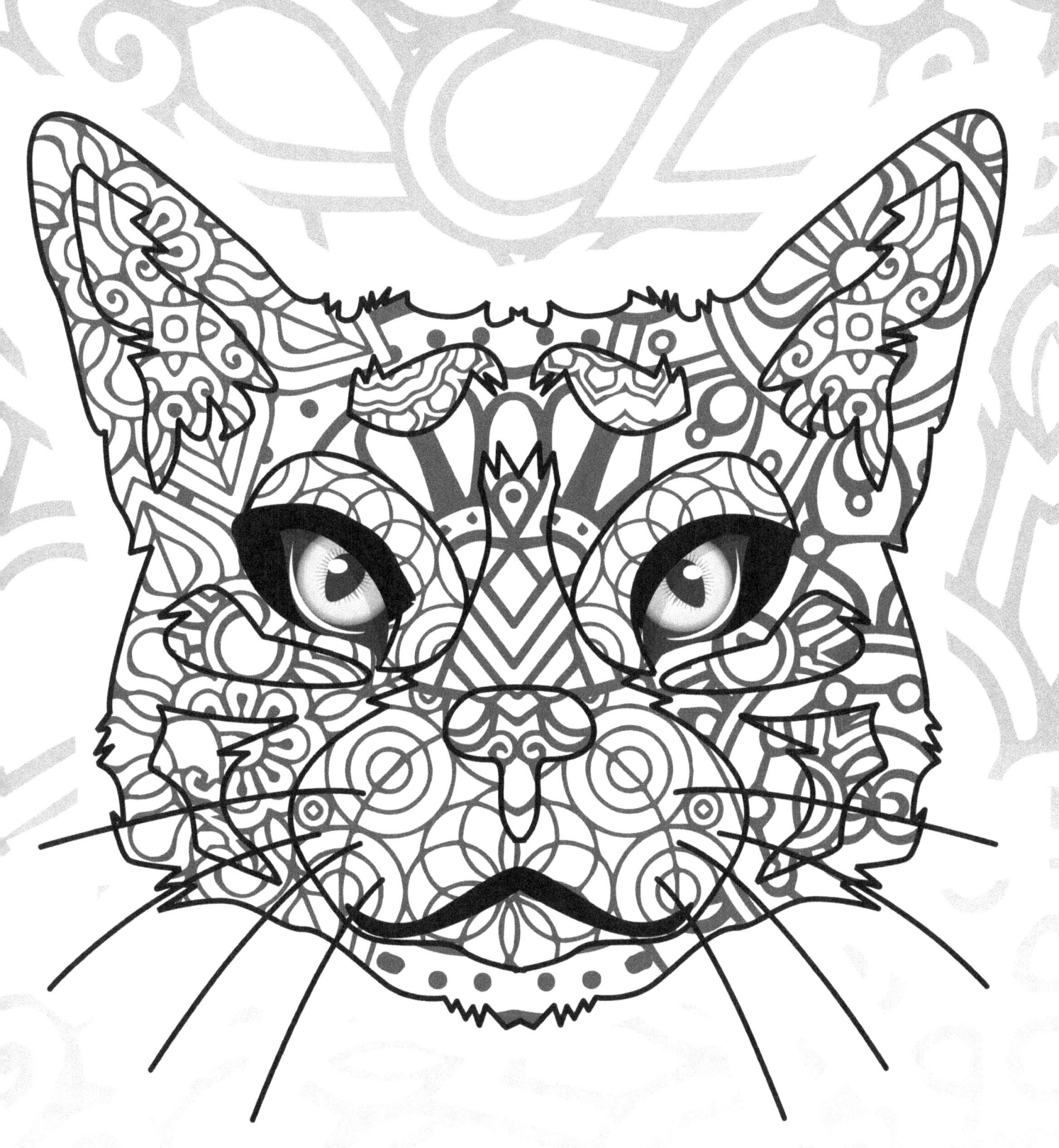

SMILE, THEN WE LOOK
FOR ONE HELL OF A REASON

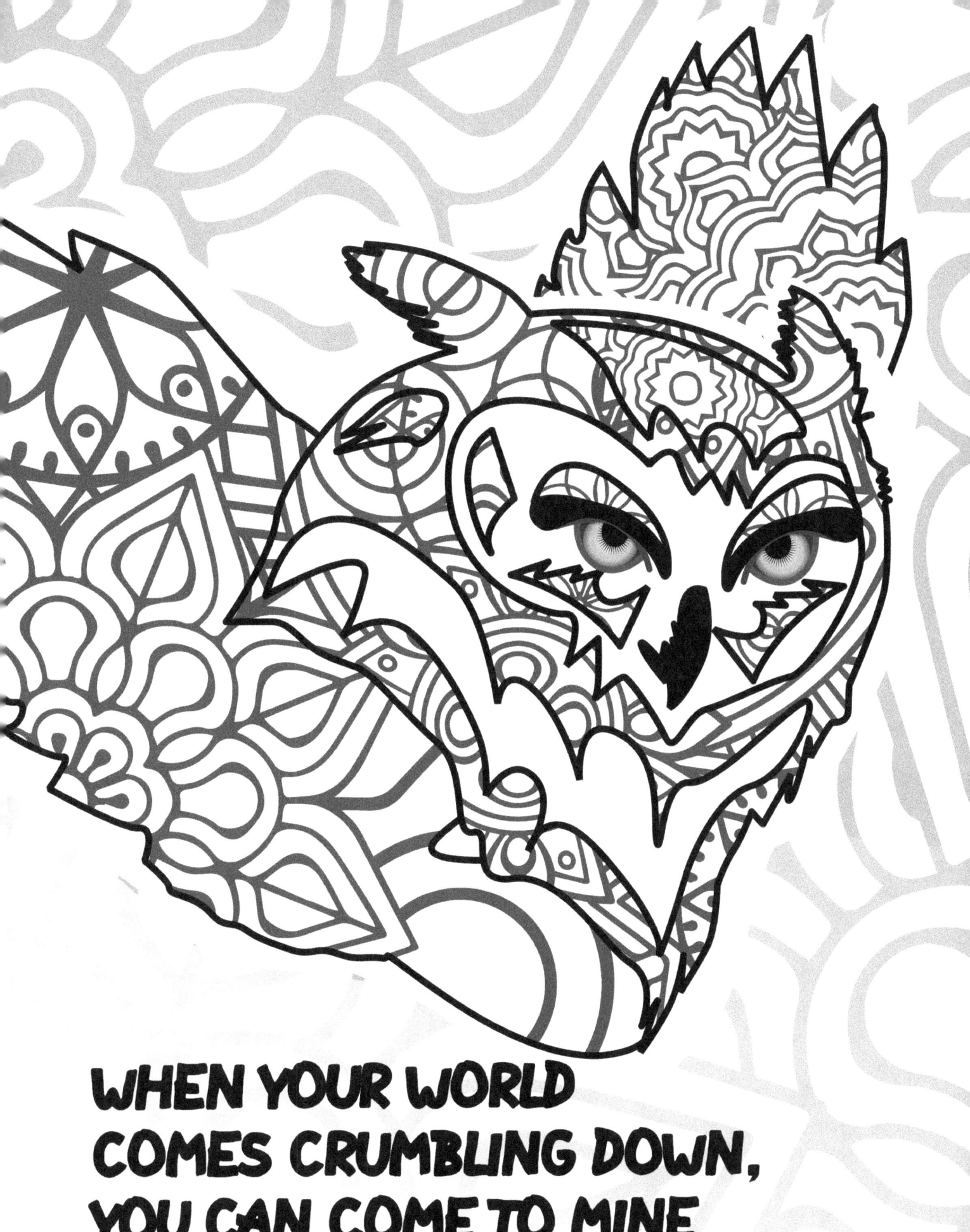

WHEN YOUR WORLD
COMES CRUMBLING DOWN,
YOU CAN COME TO MINE

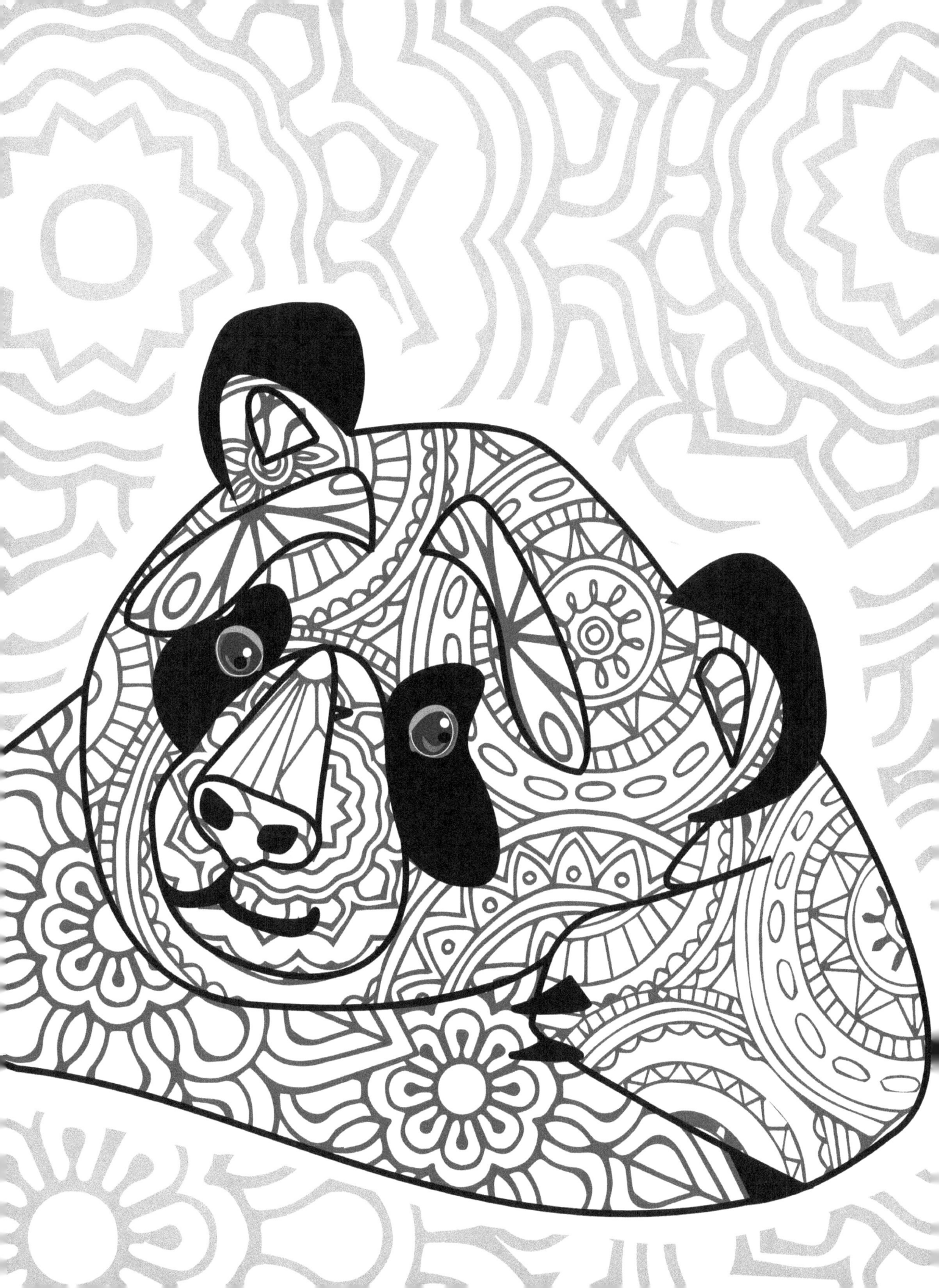

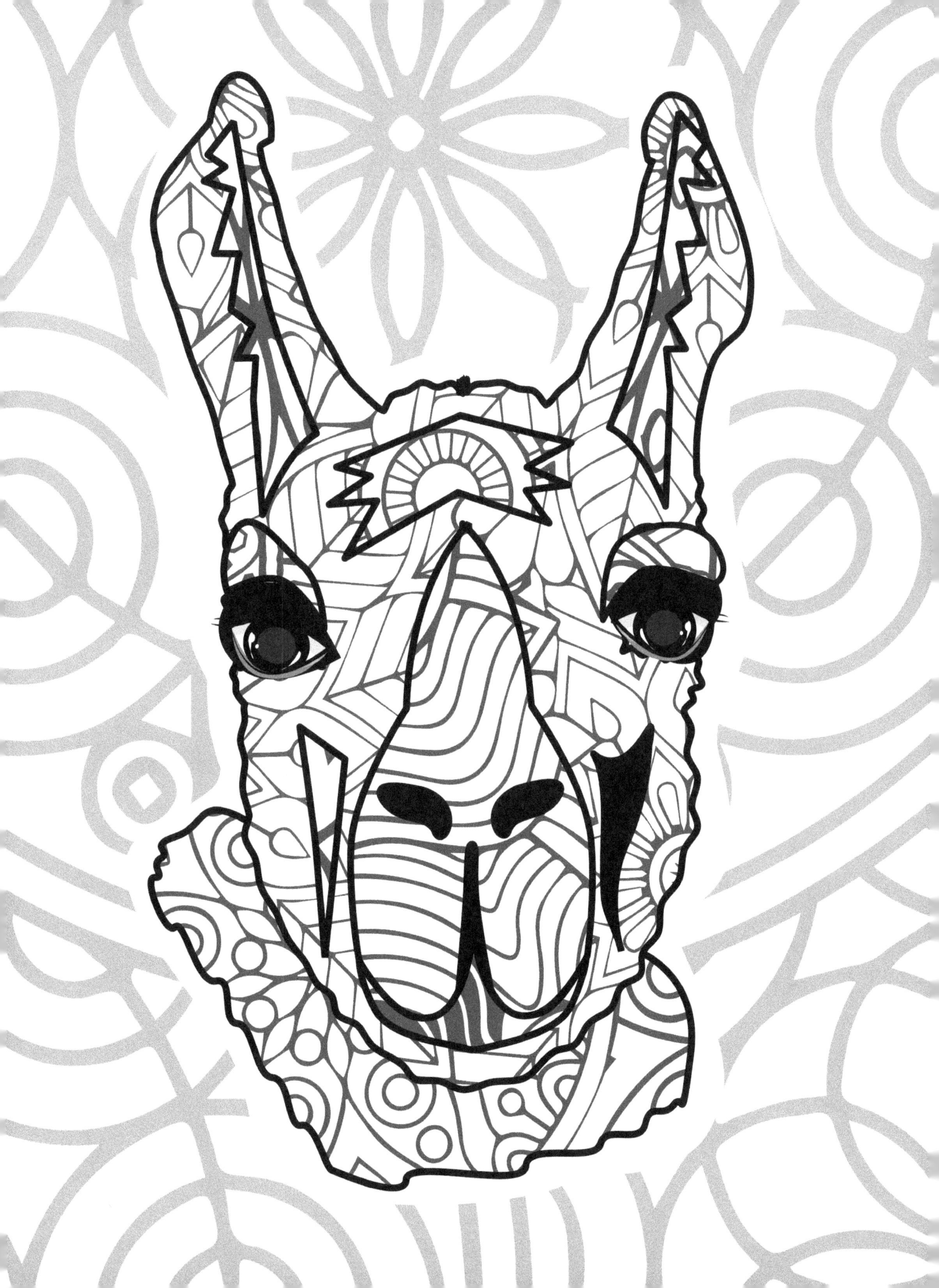

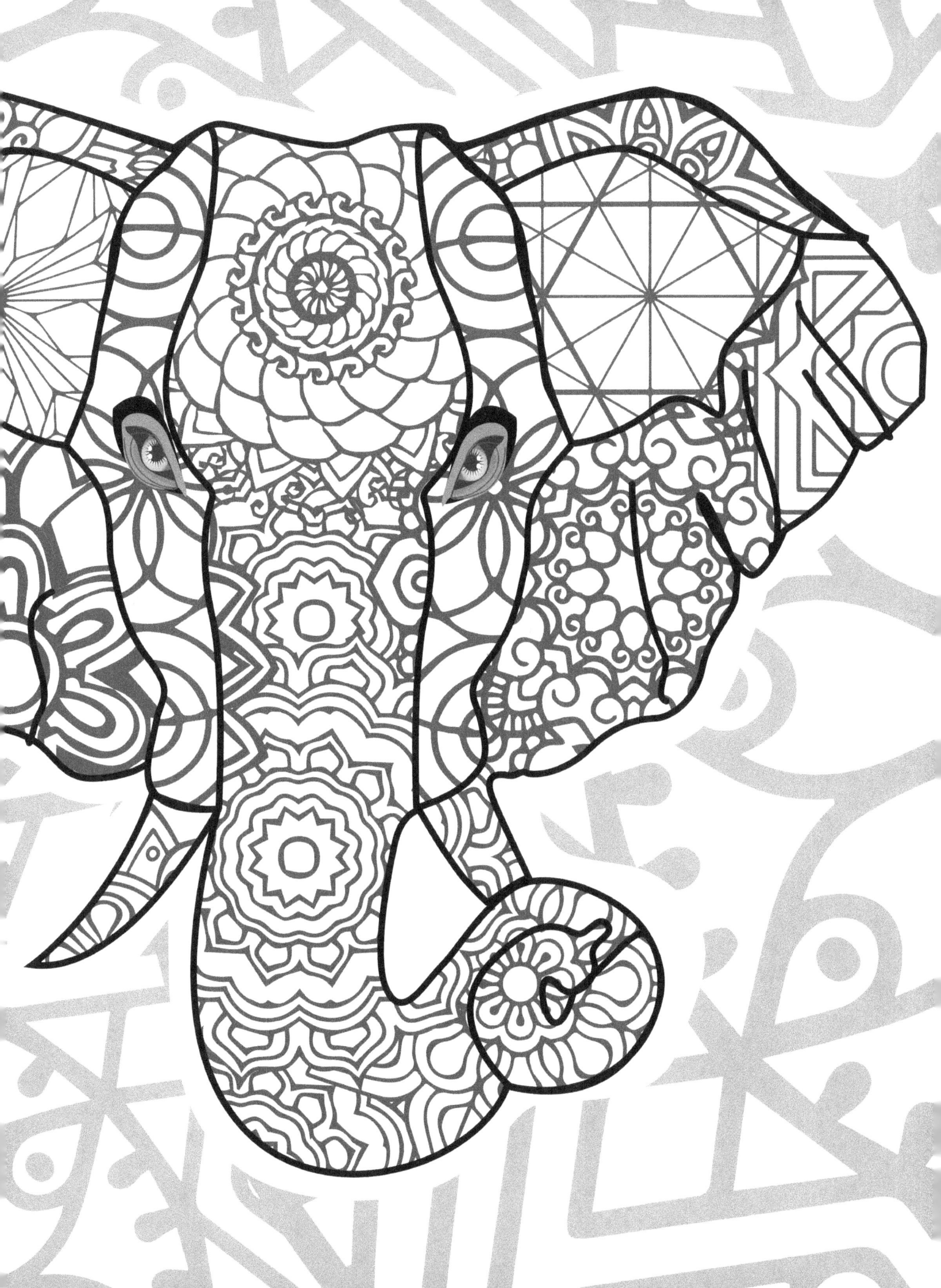

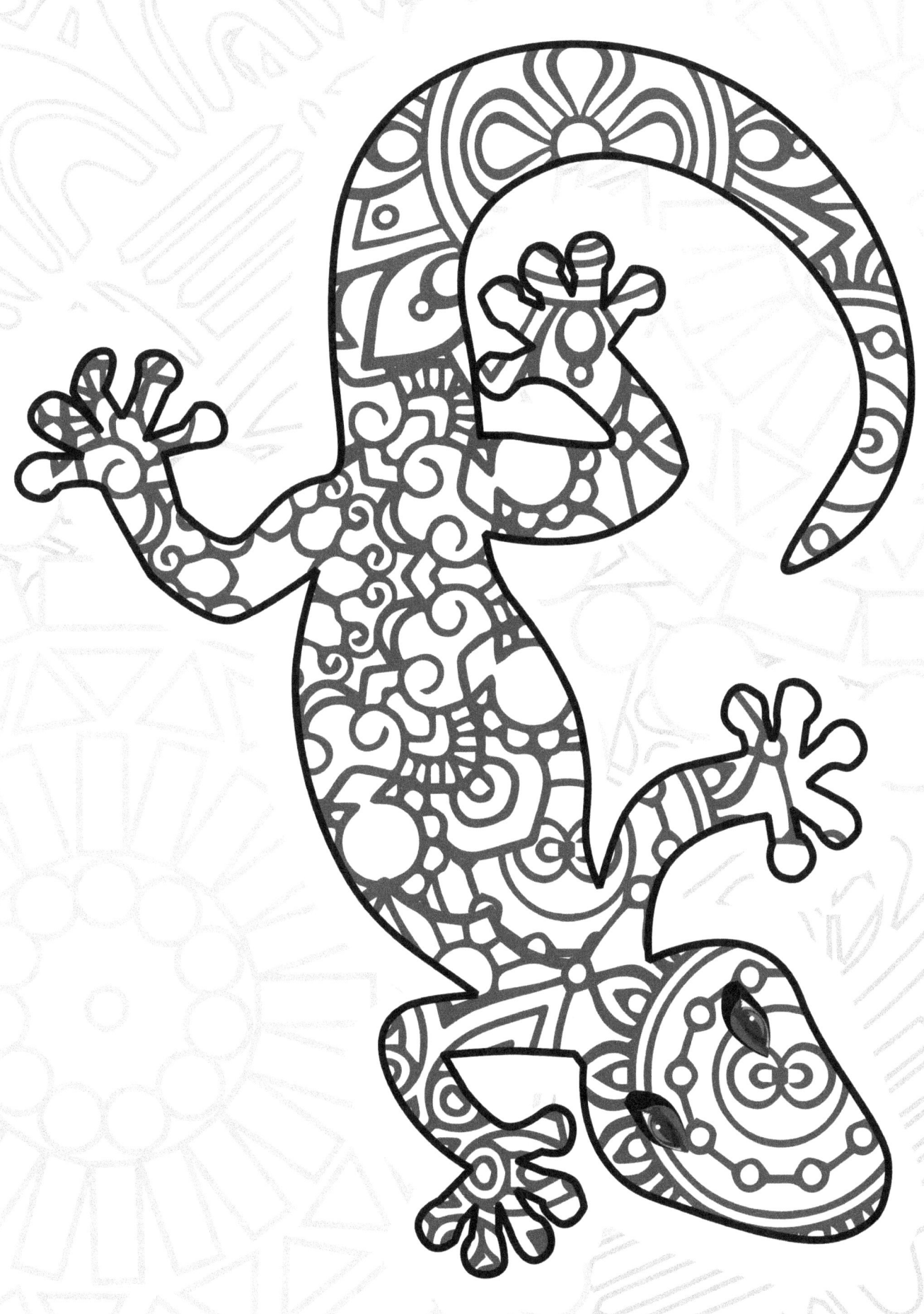

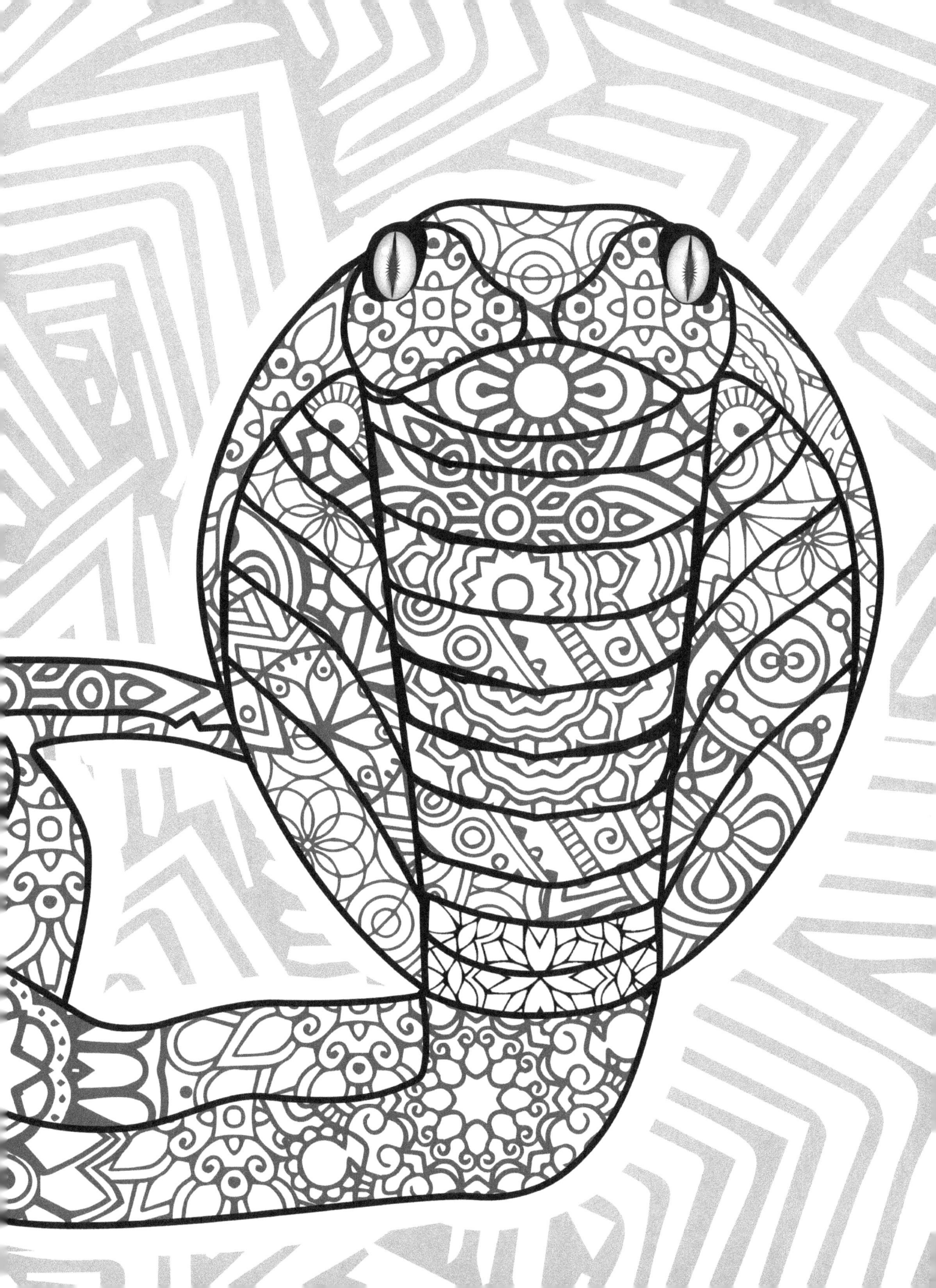

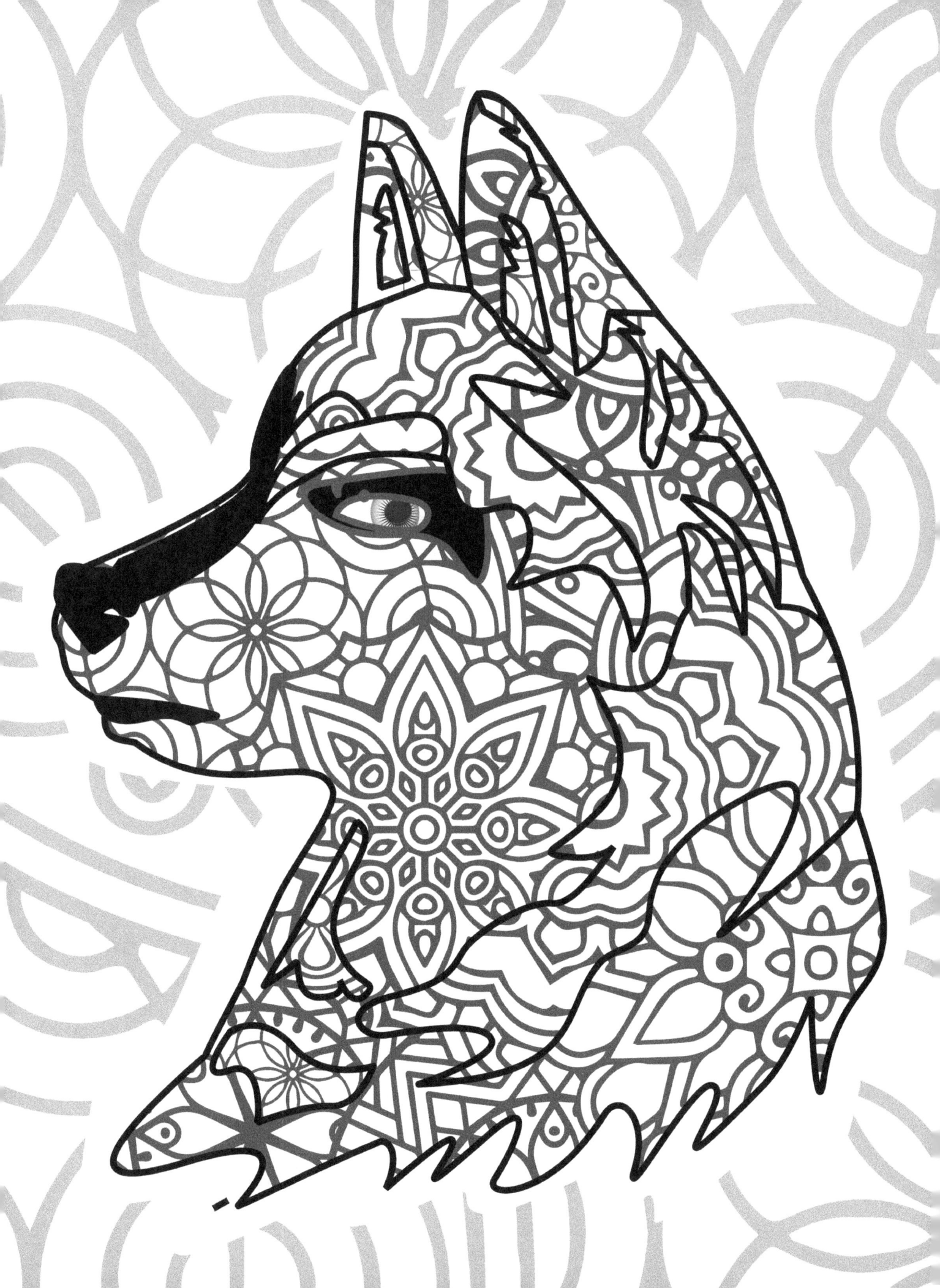

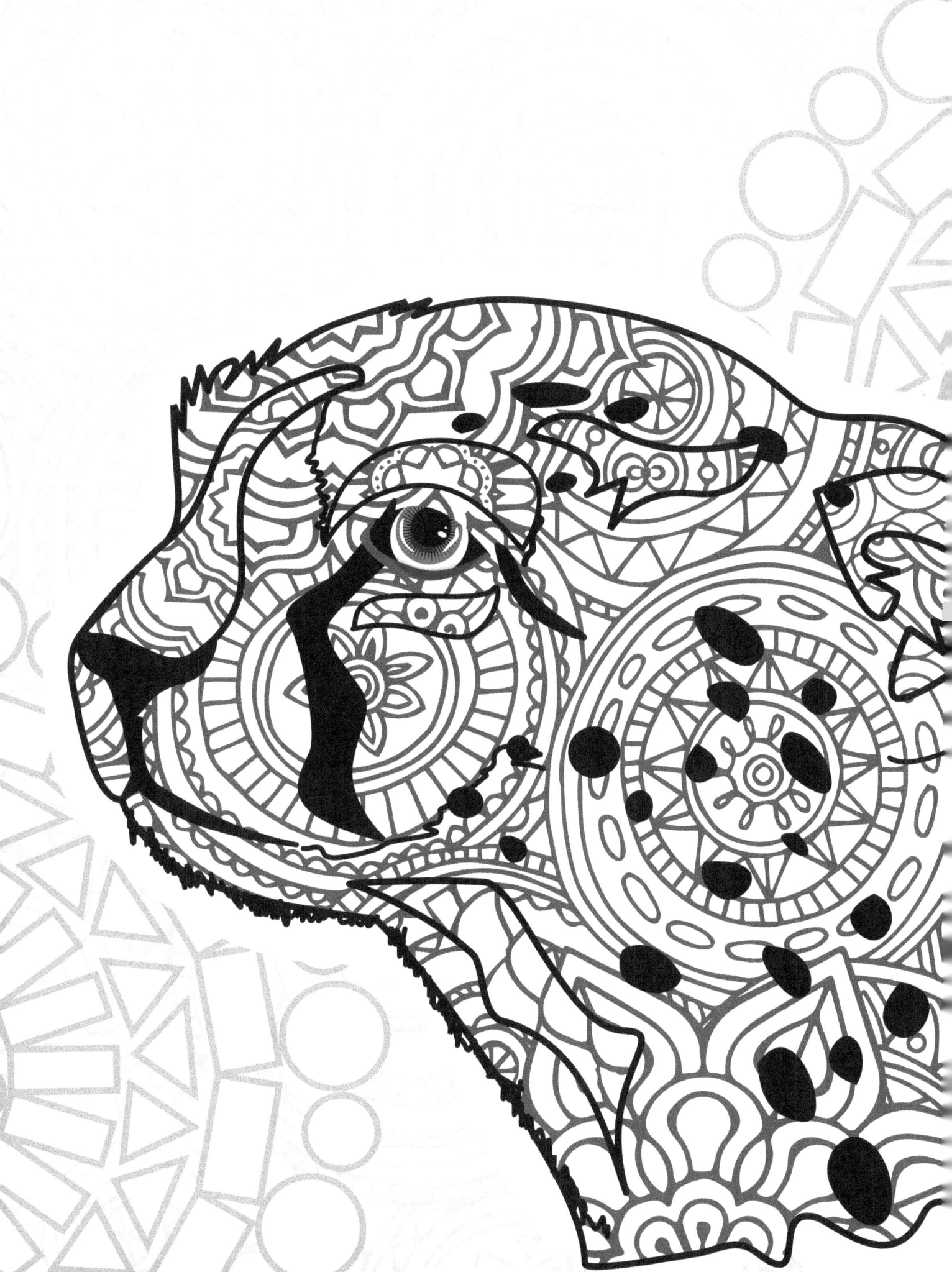

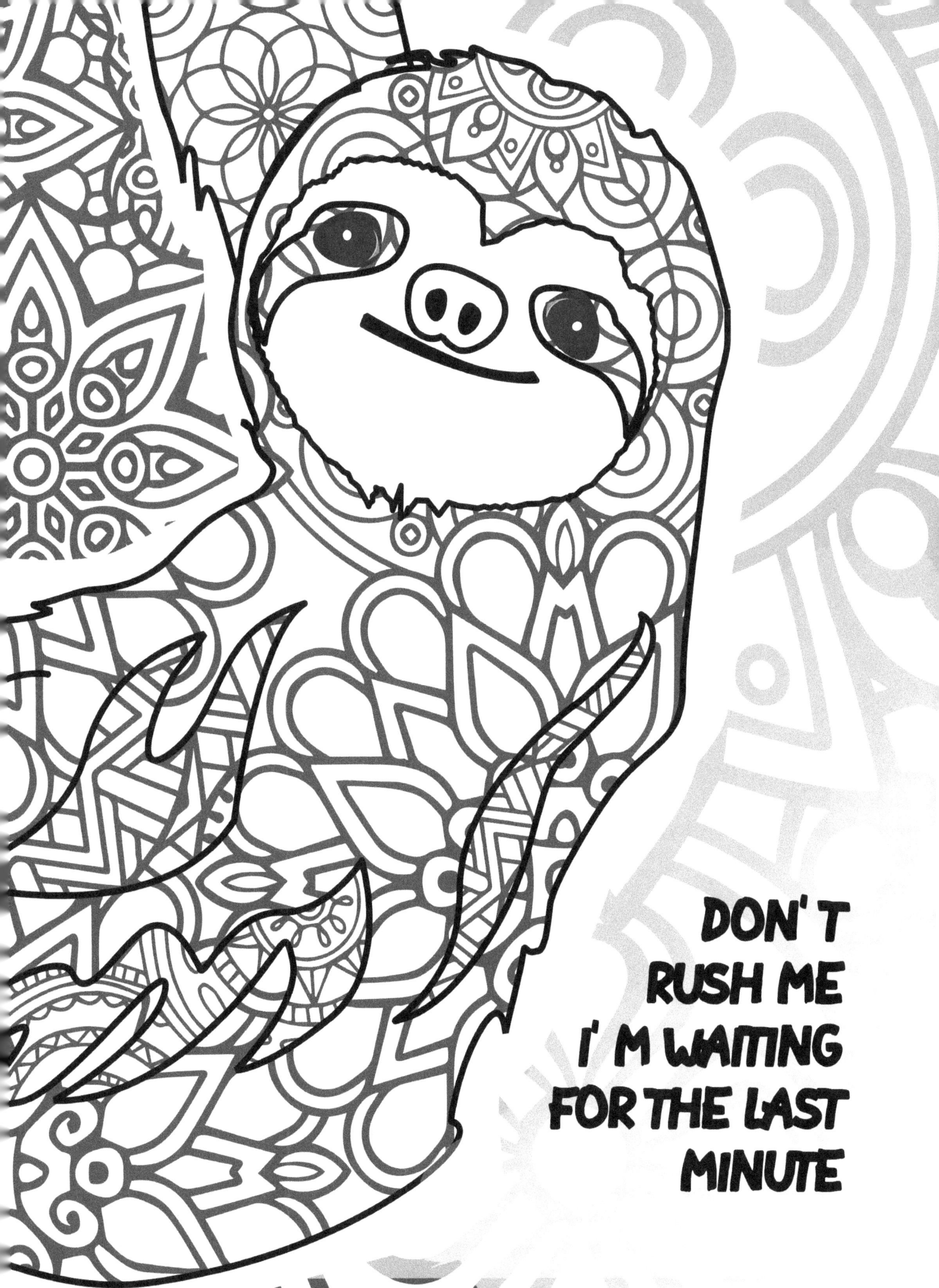

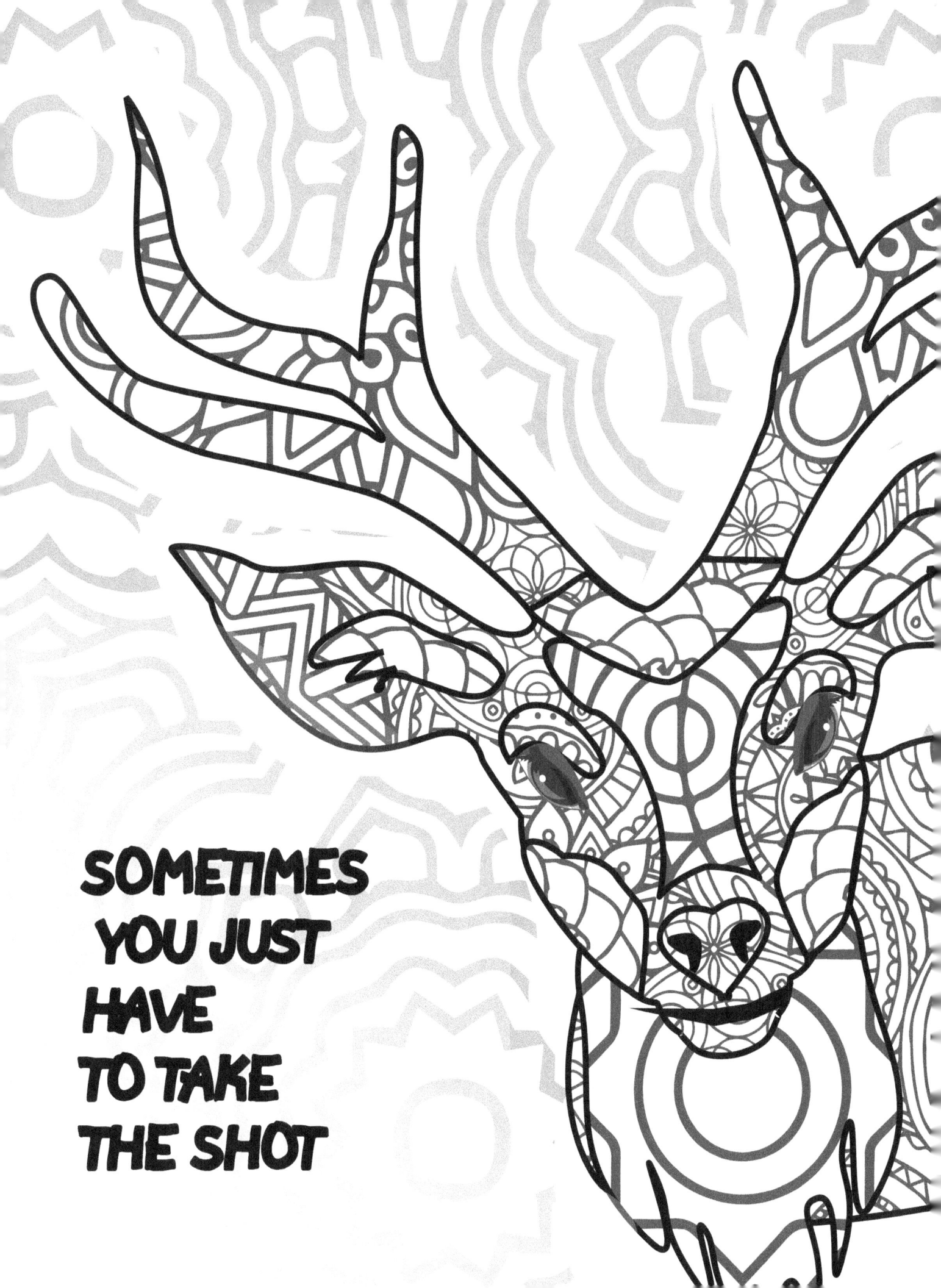

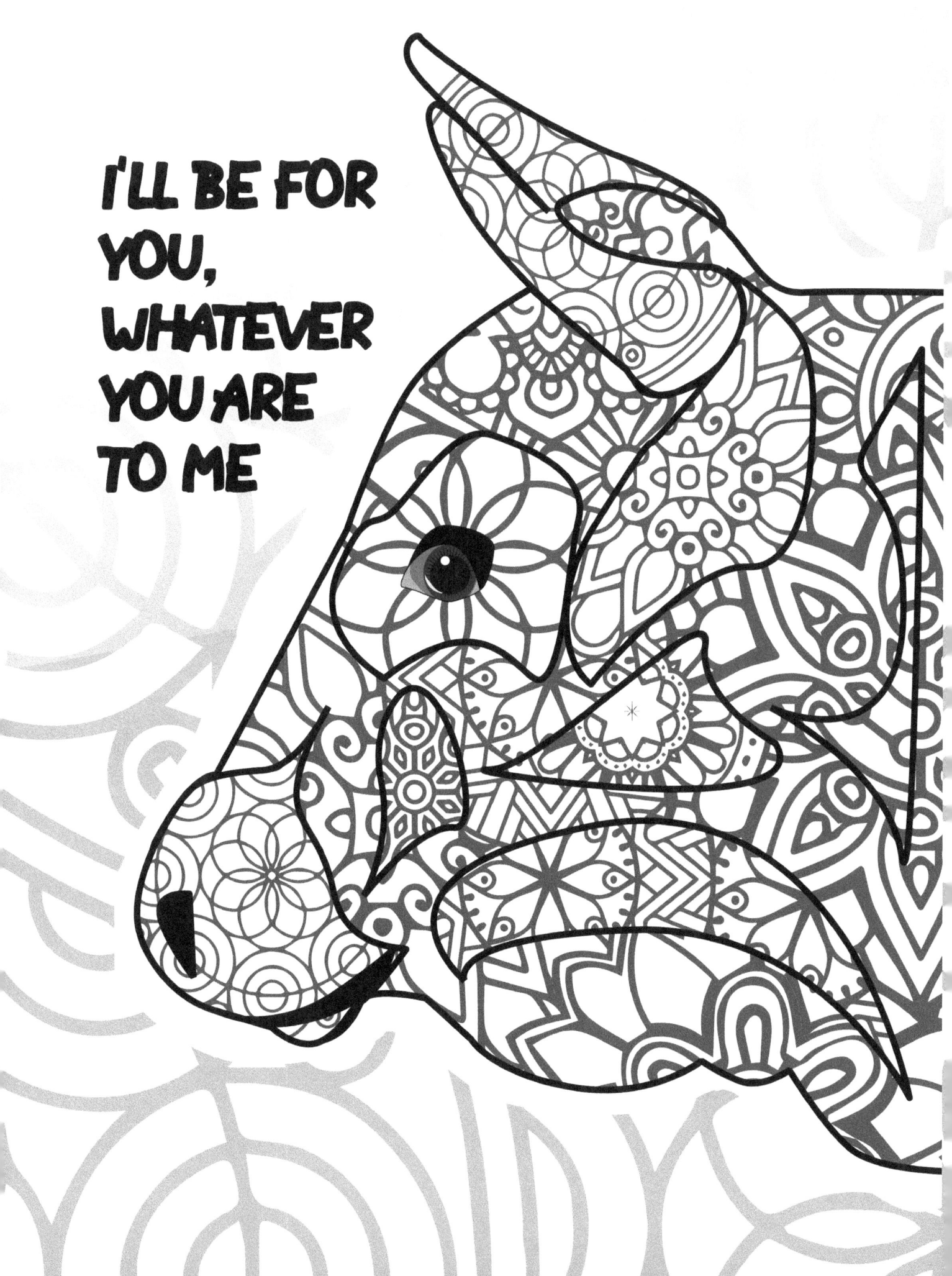

I'LL BE FOR YOU, WHATEVER YOU ARE TO ME

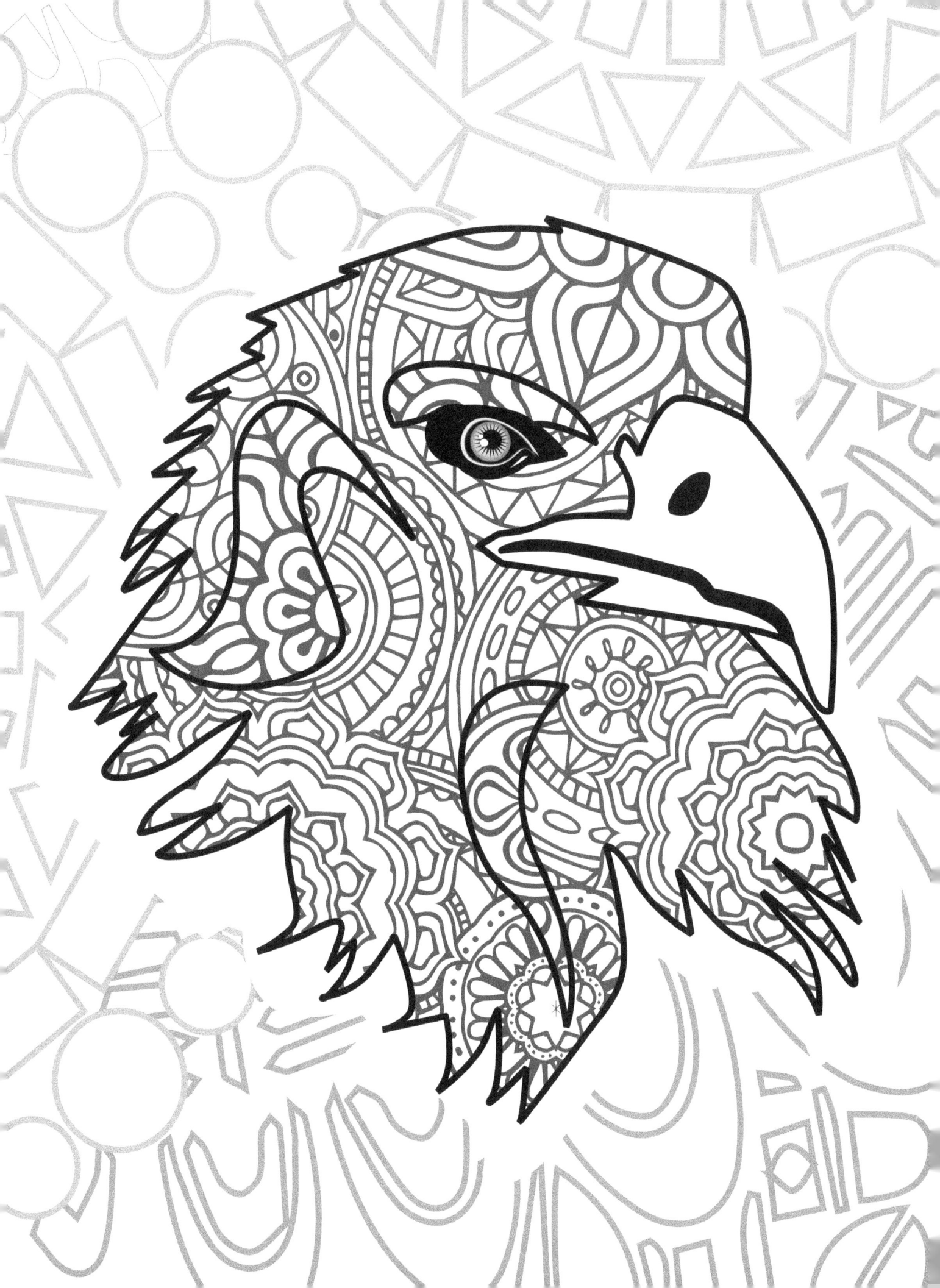

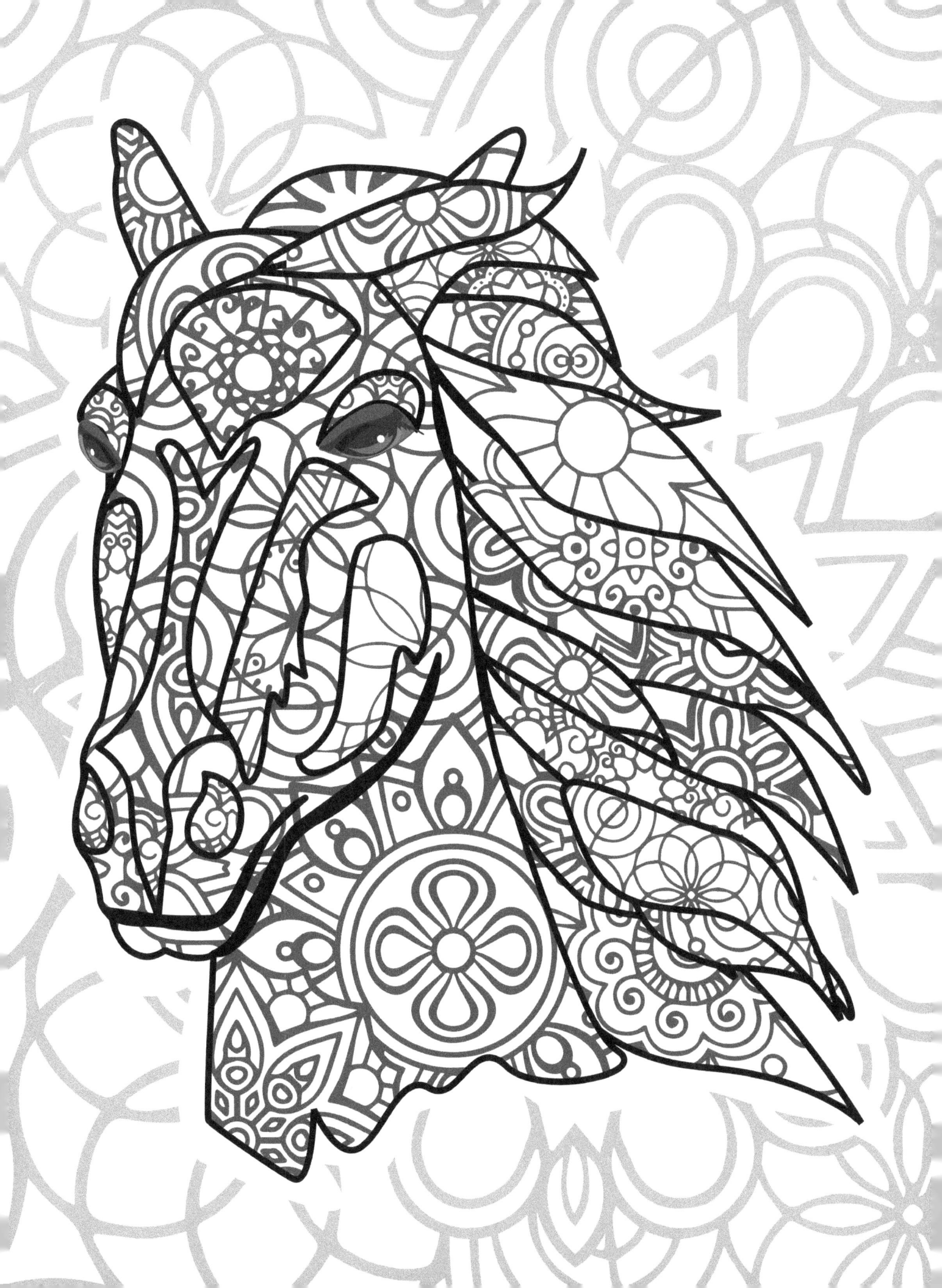

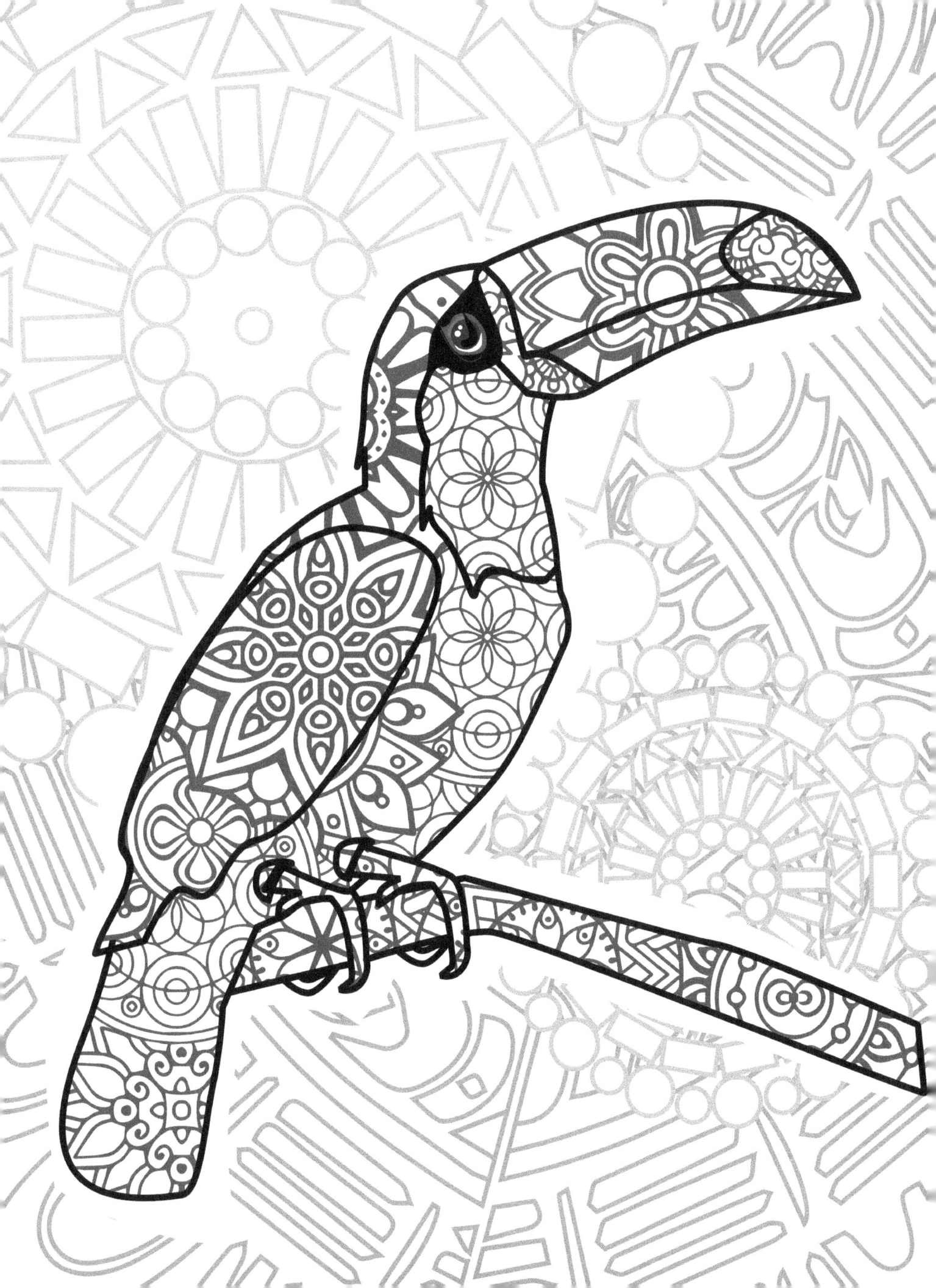

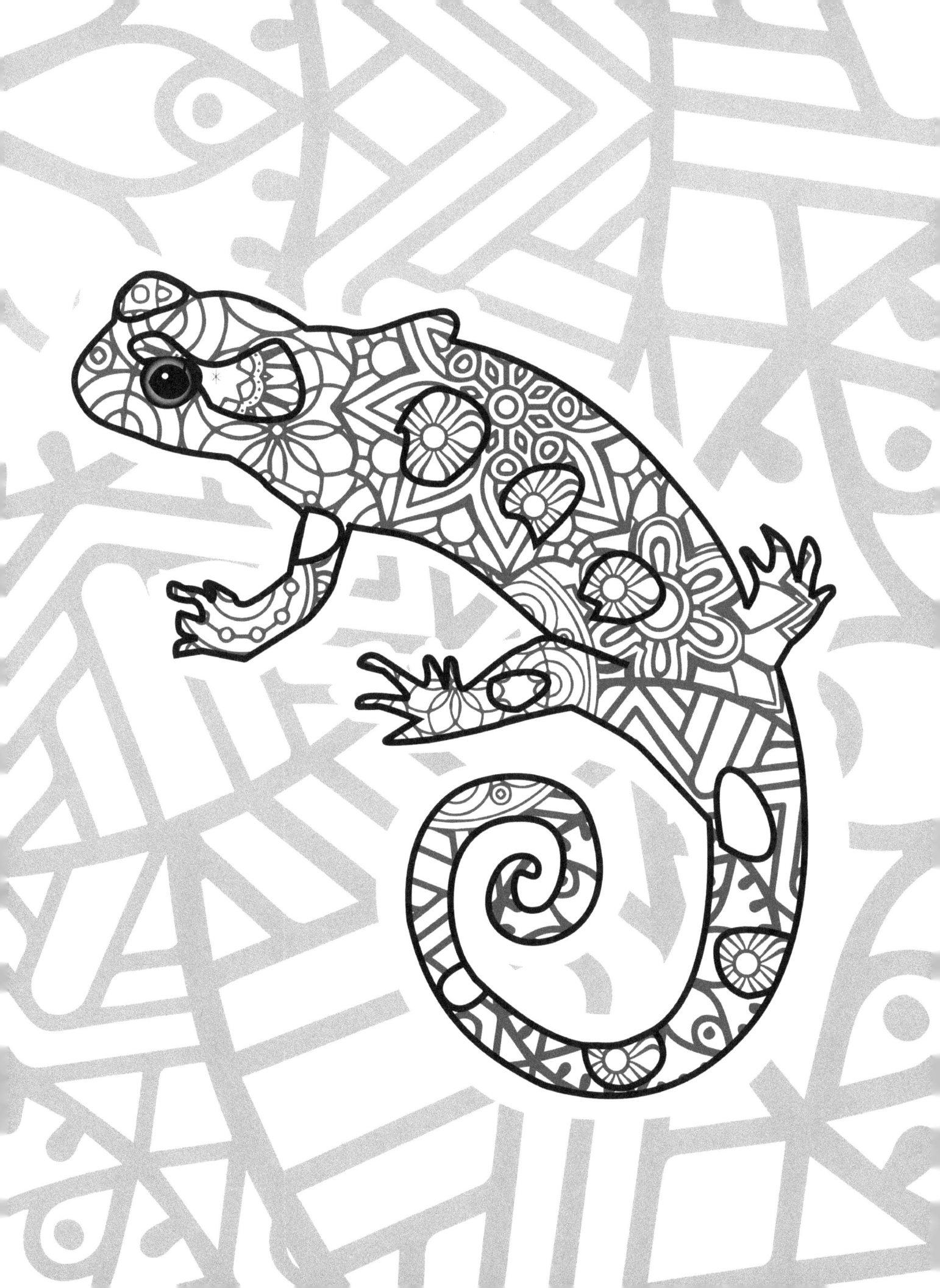

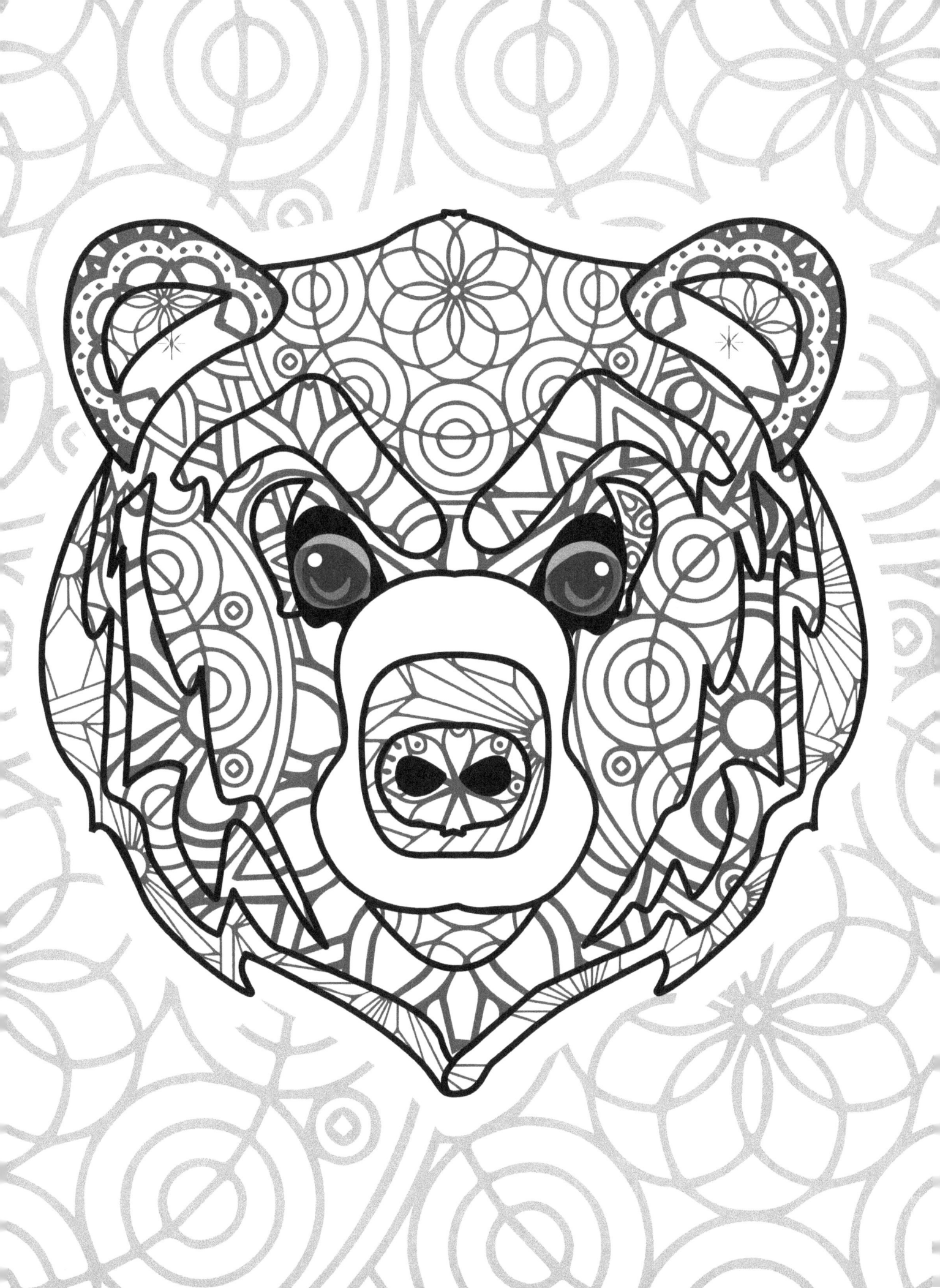

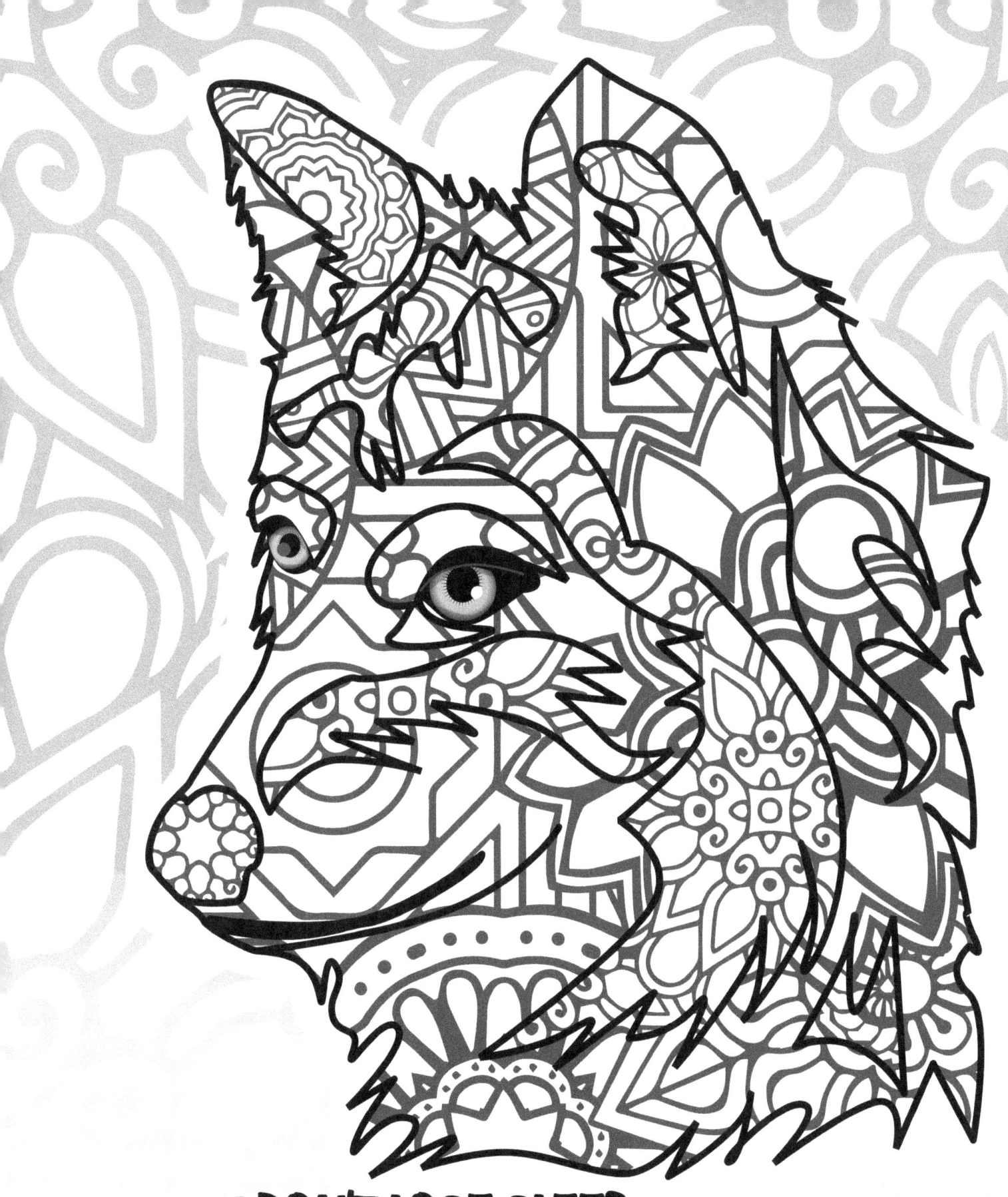

I DON'T LOSE SLEEP
DUE TO THE OPINION OF SHEEP

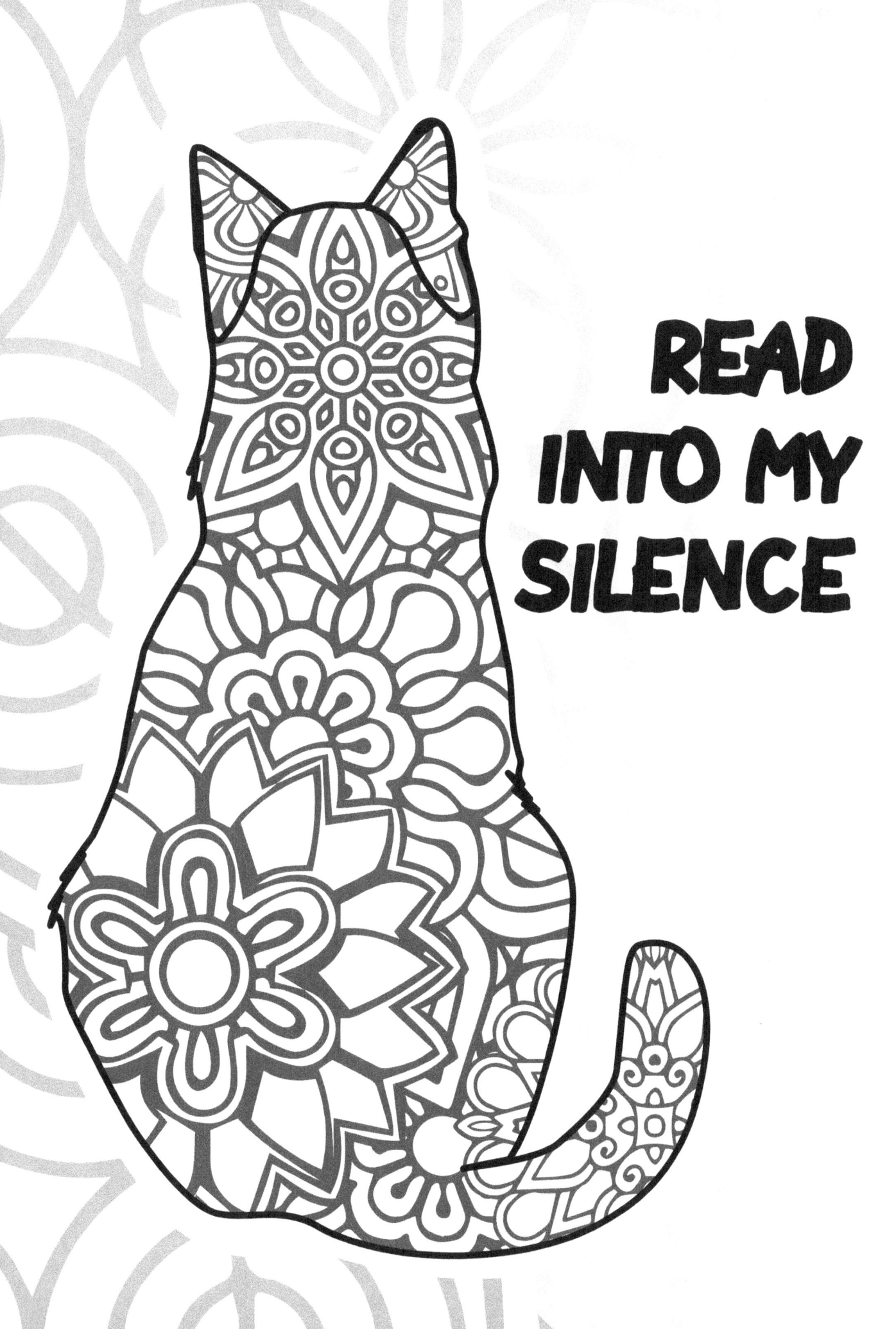

READ
INTO MY
SILENCE

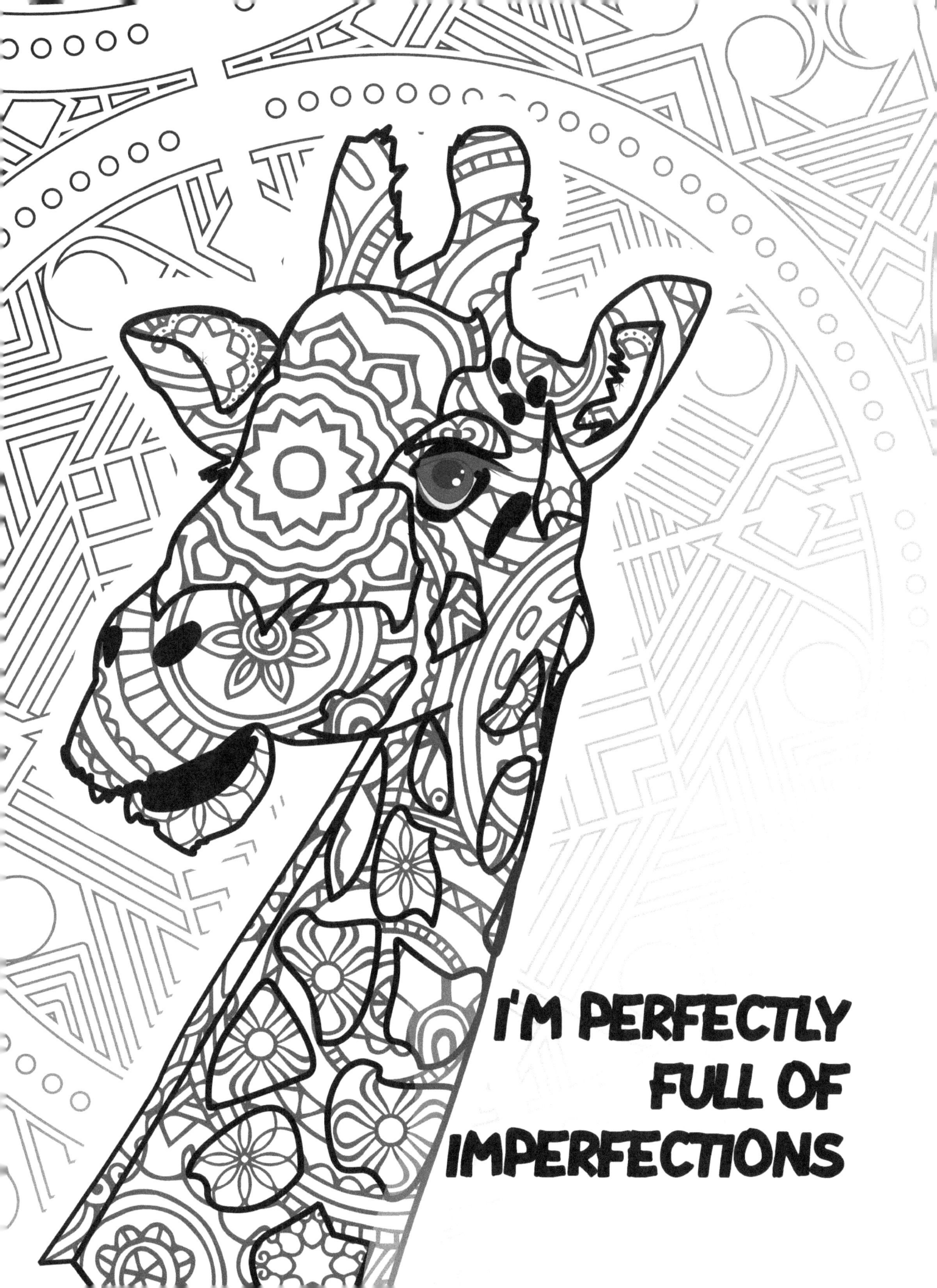

I'M PERFECTLY
FULL OF
IMPERFECTIONS

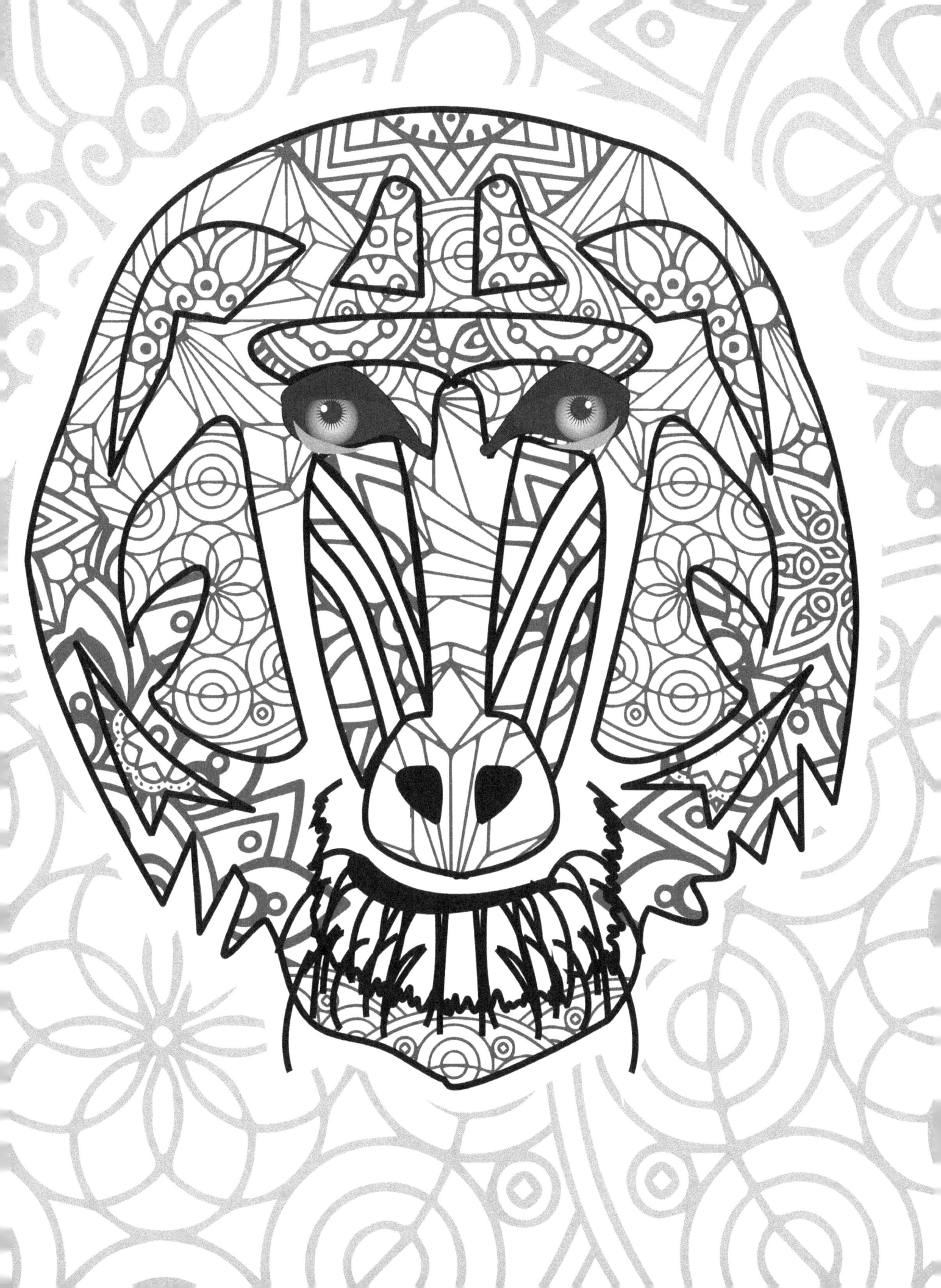

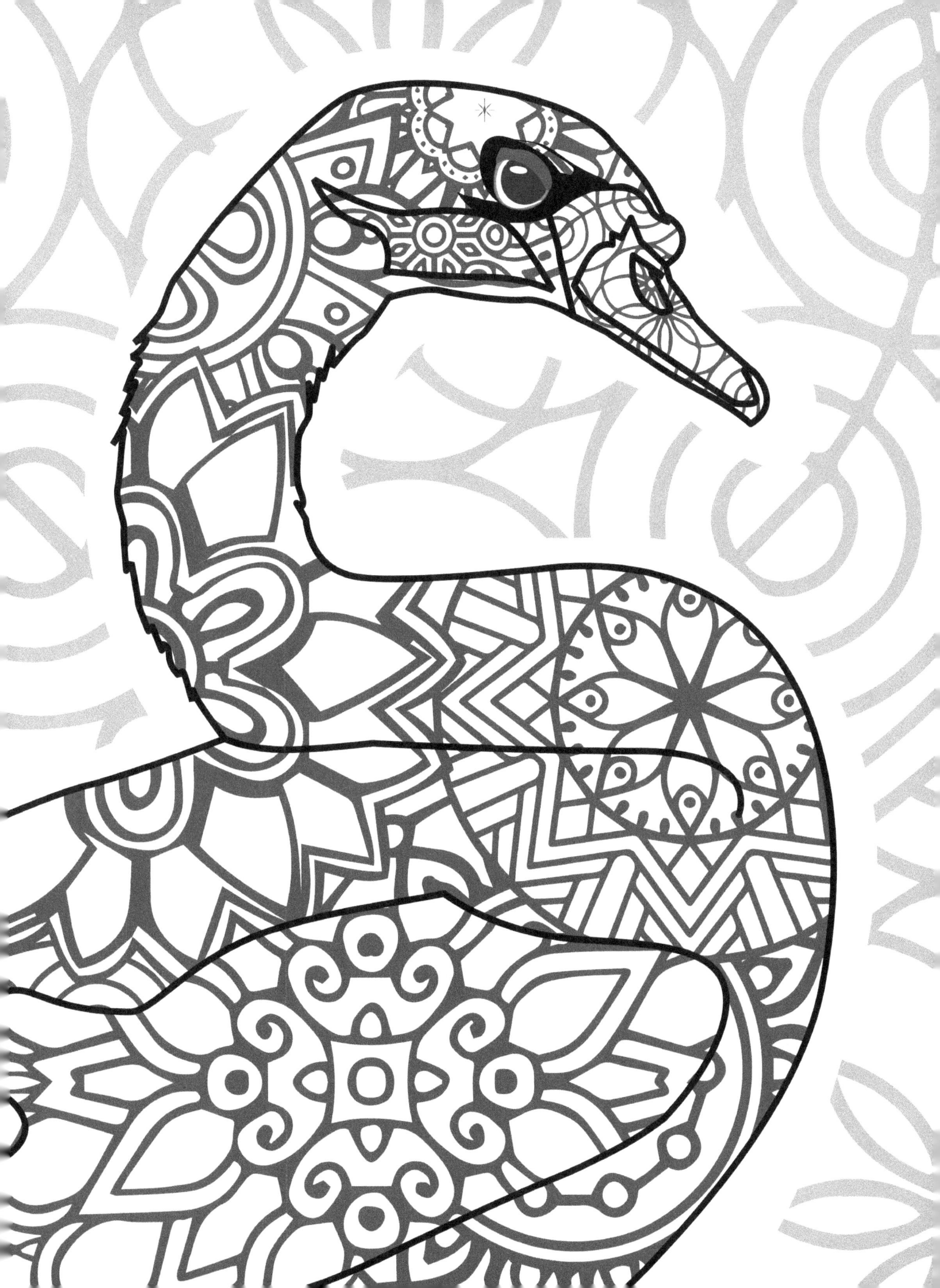

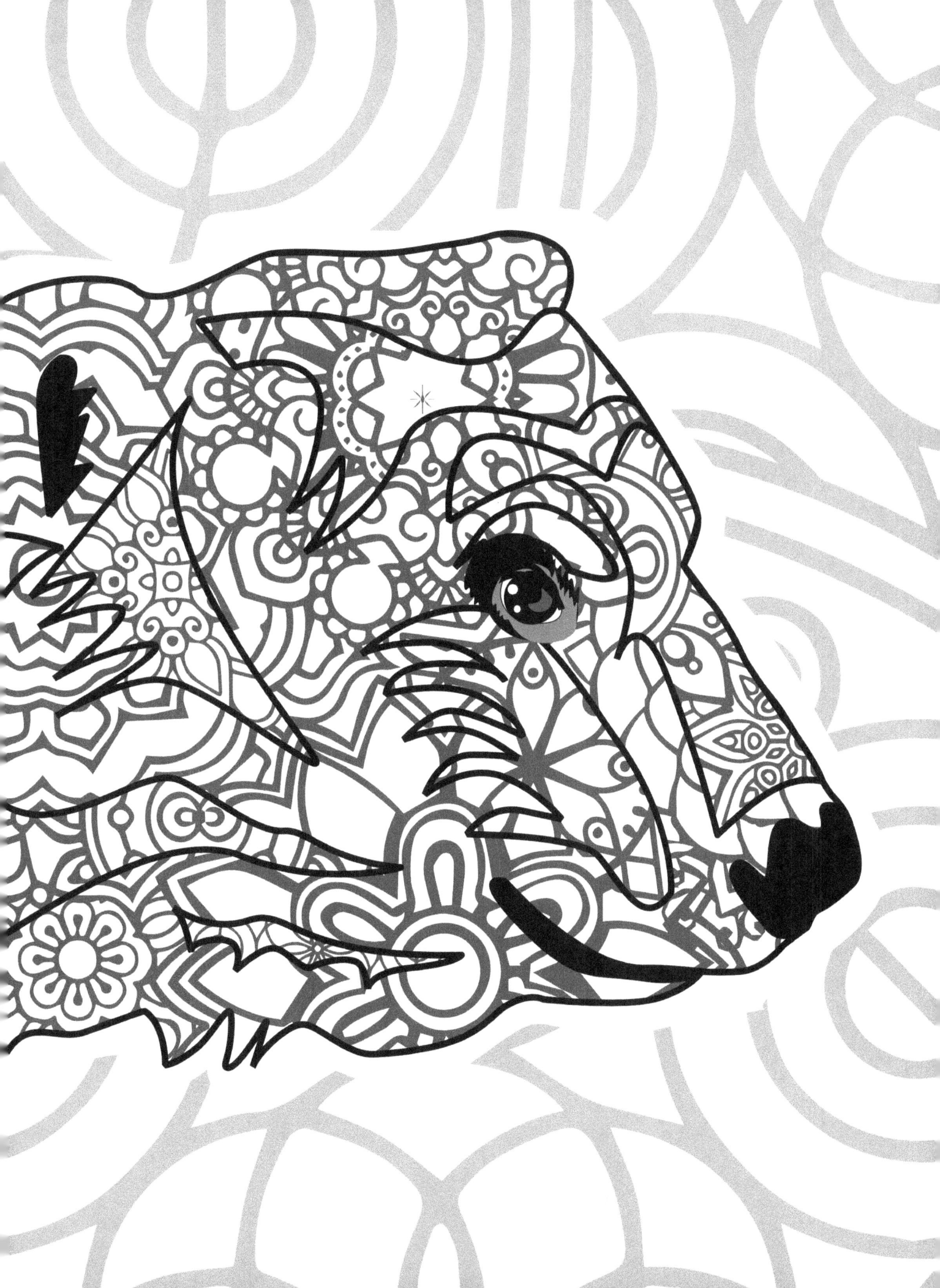

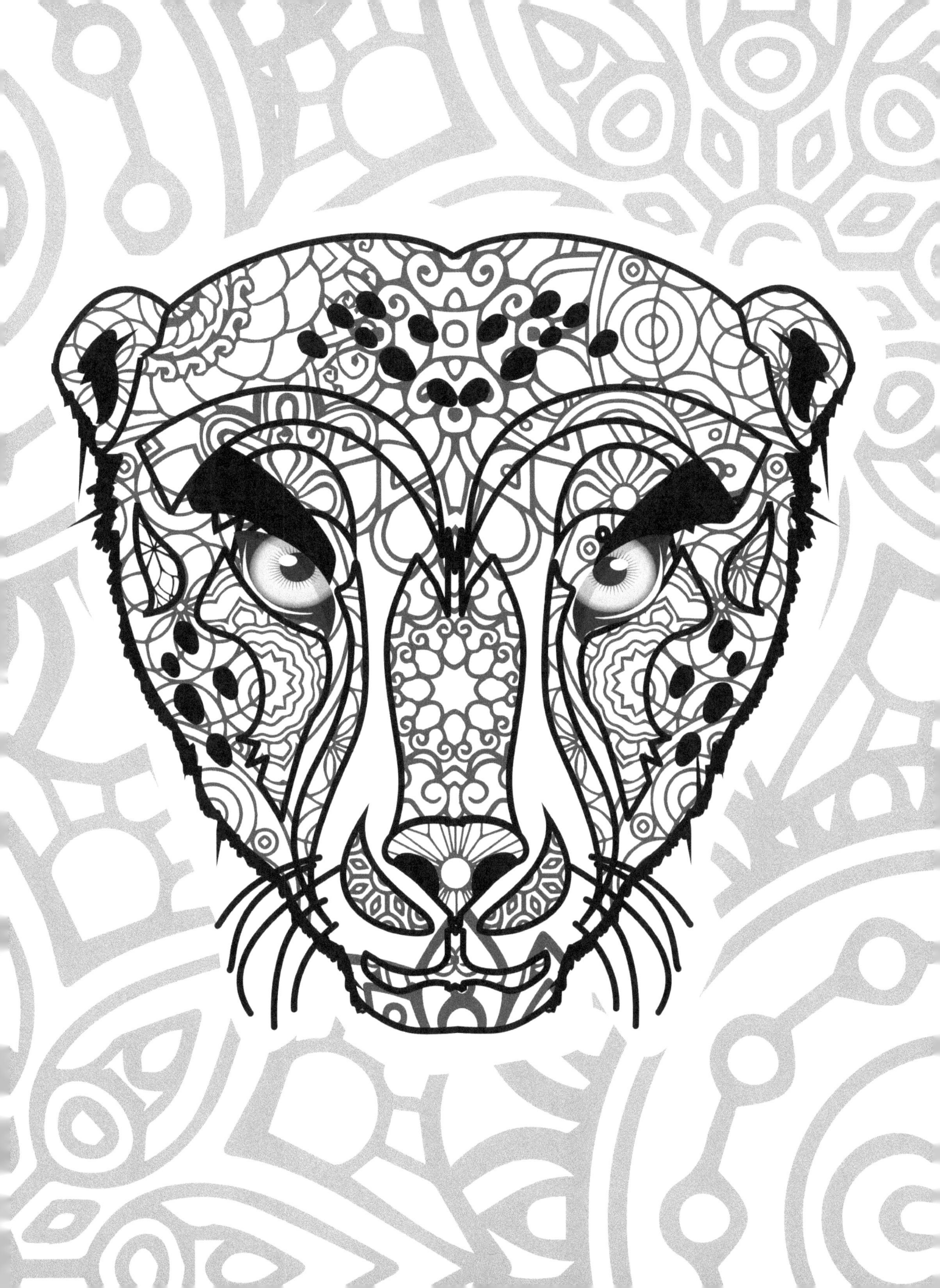

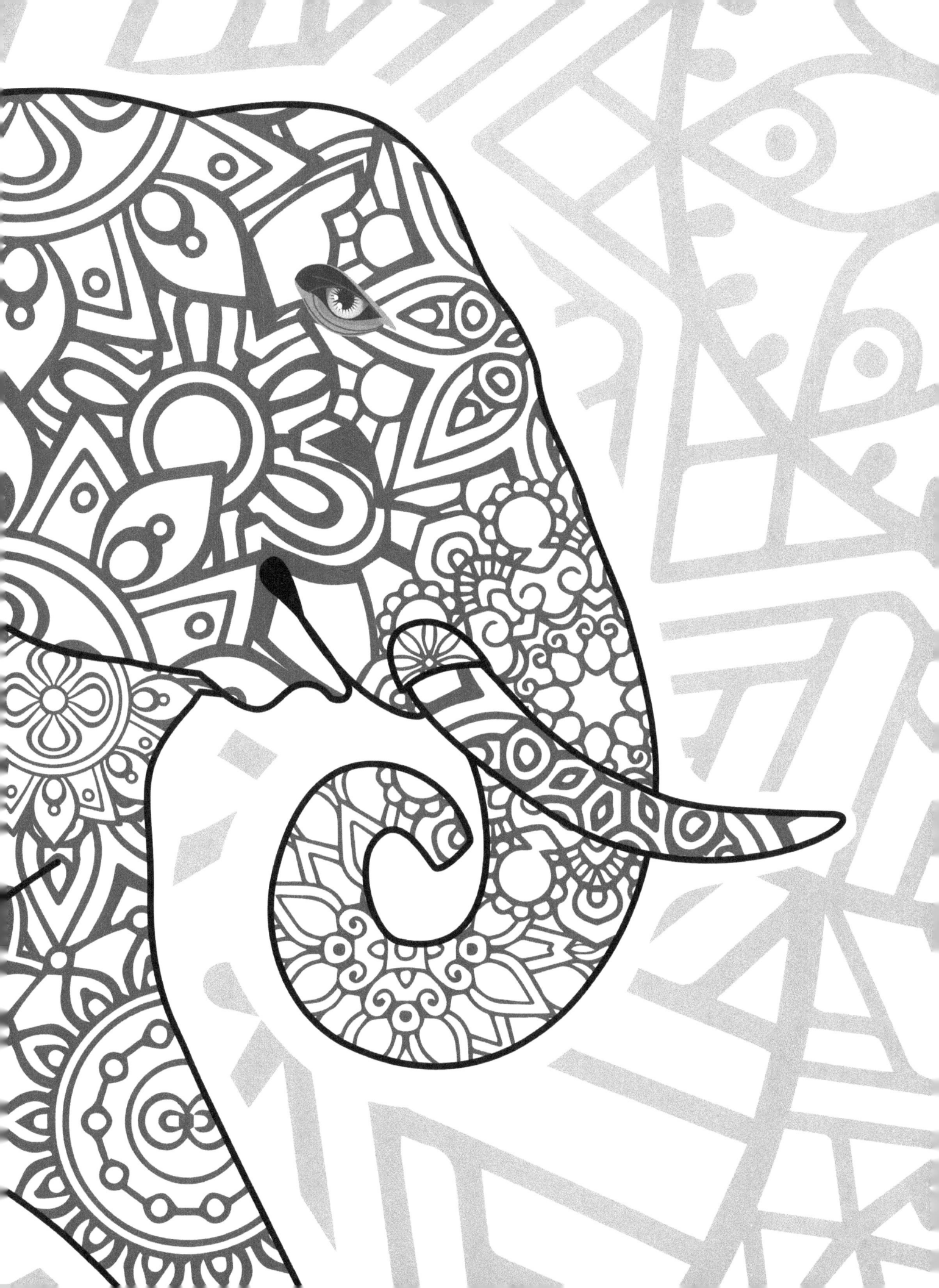

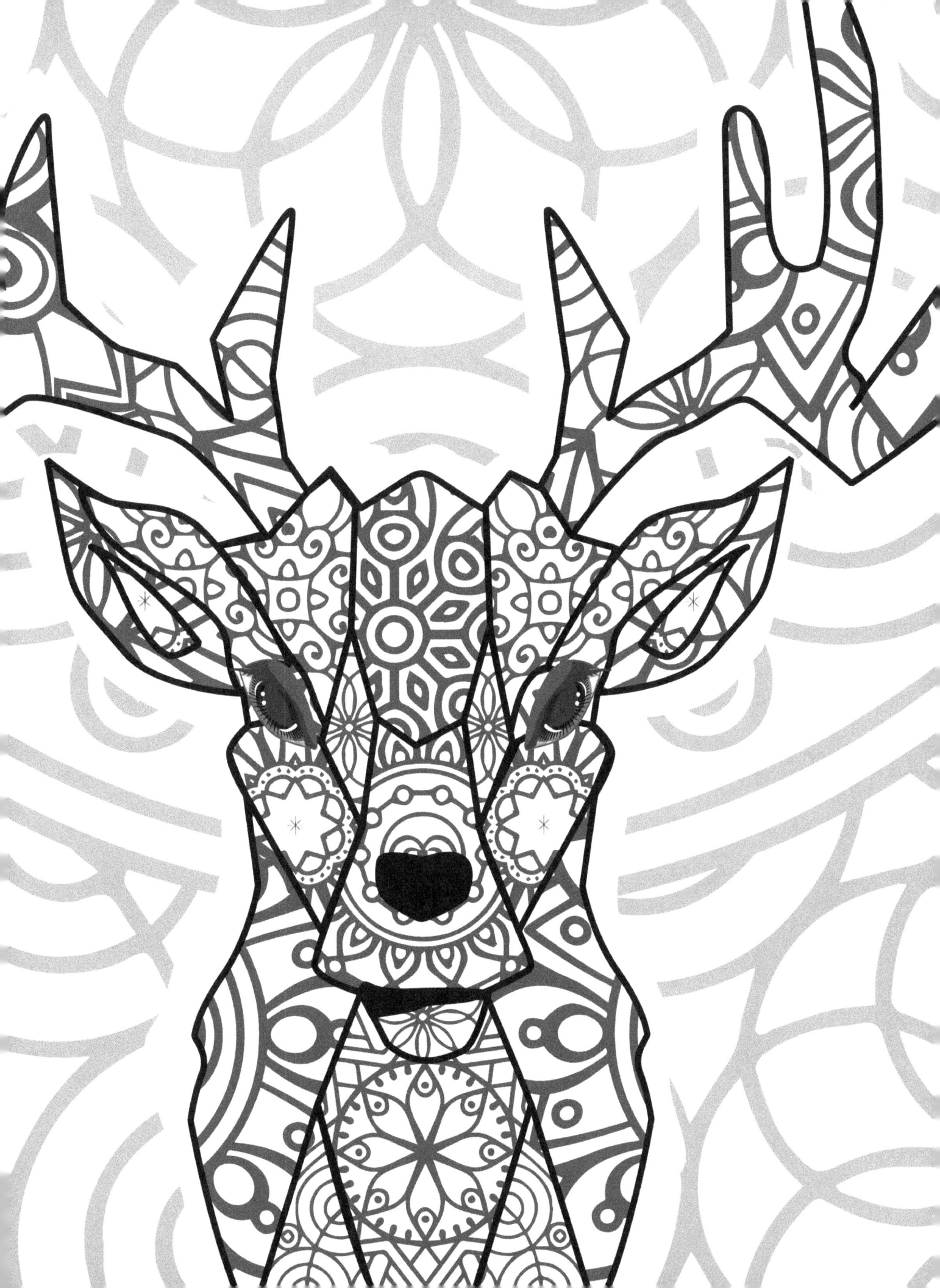

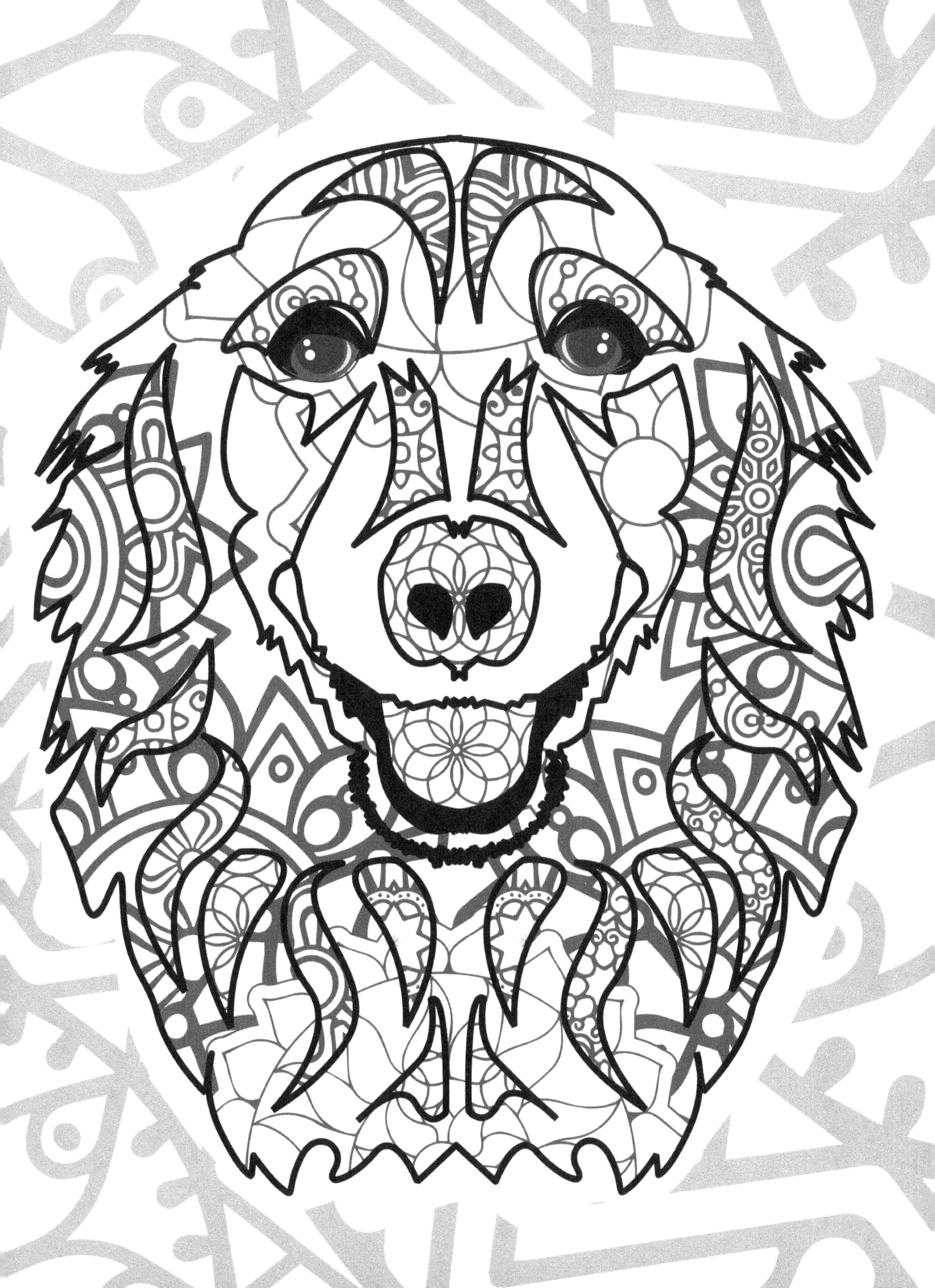

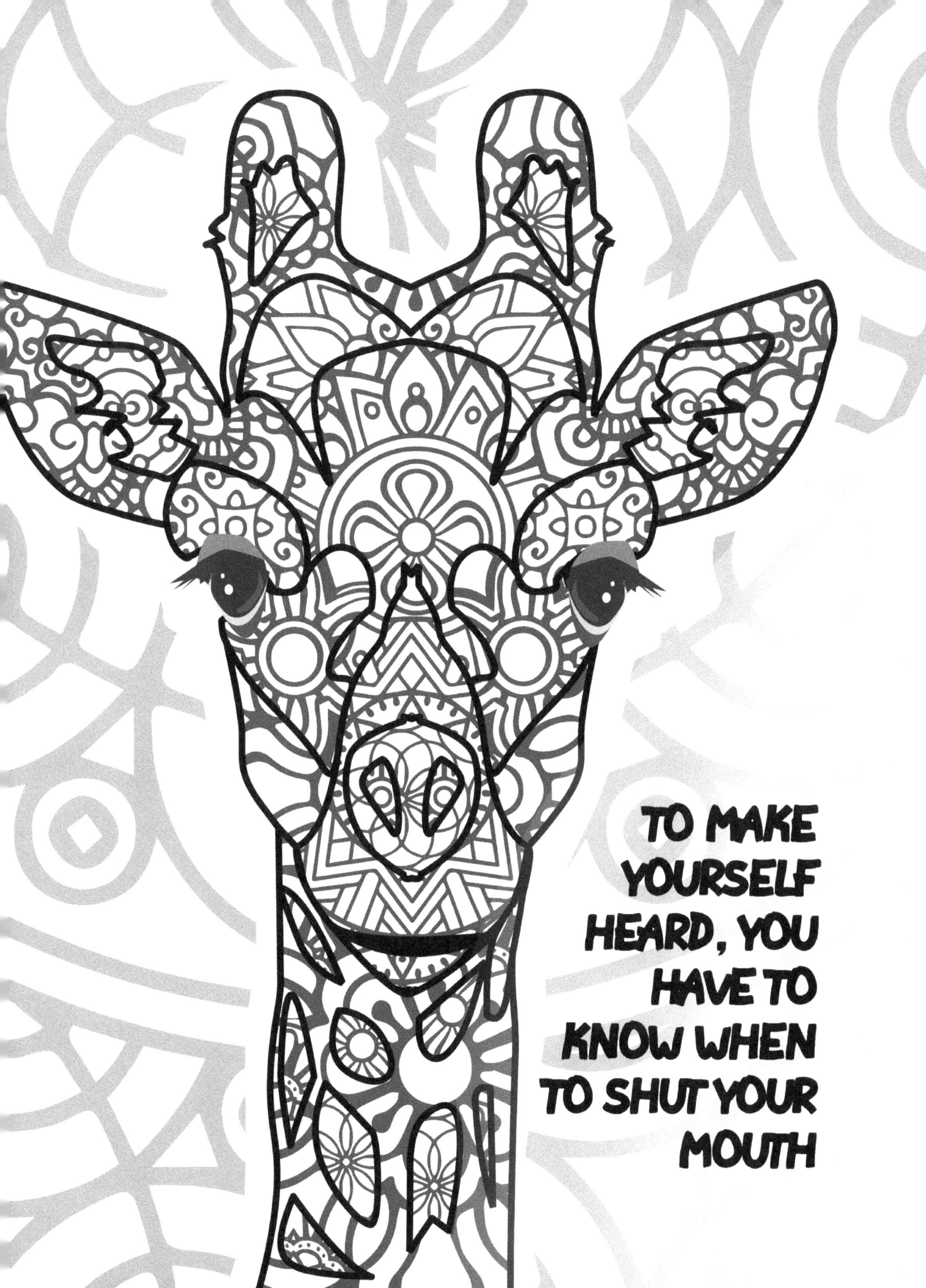

TO MAKE YOURSELF HEARD, YOU HAVE TO KNOW WHEN TO SHUT YOUR MOUTH

DON'T CLARIFY IT, YOU'LL JUST MAKE IT DARKER

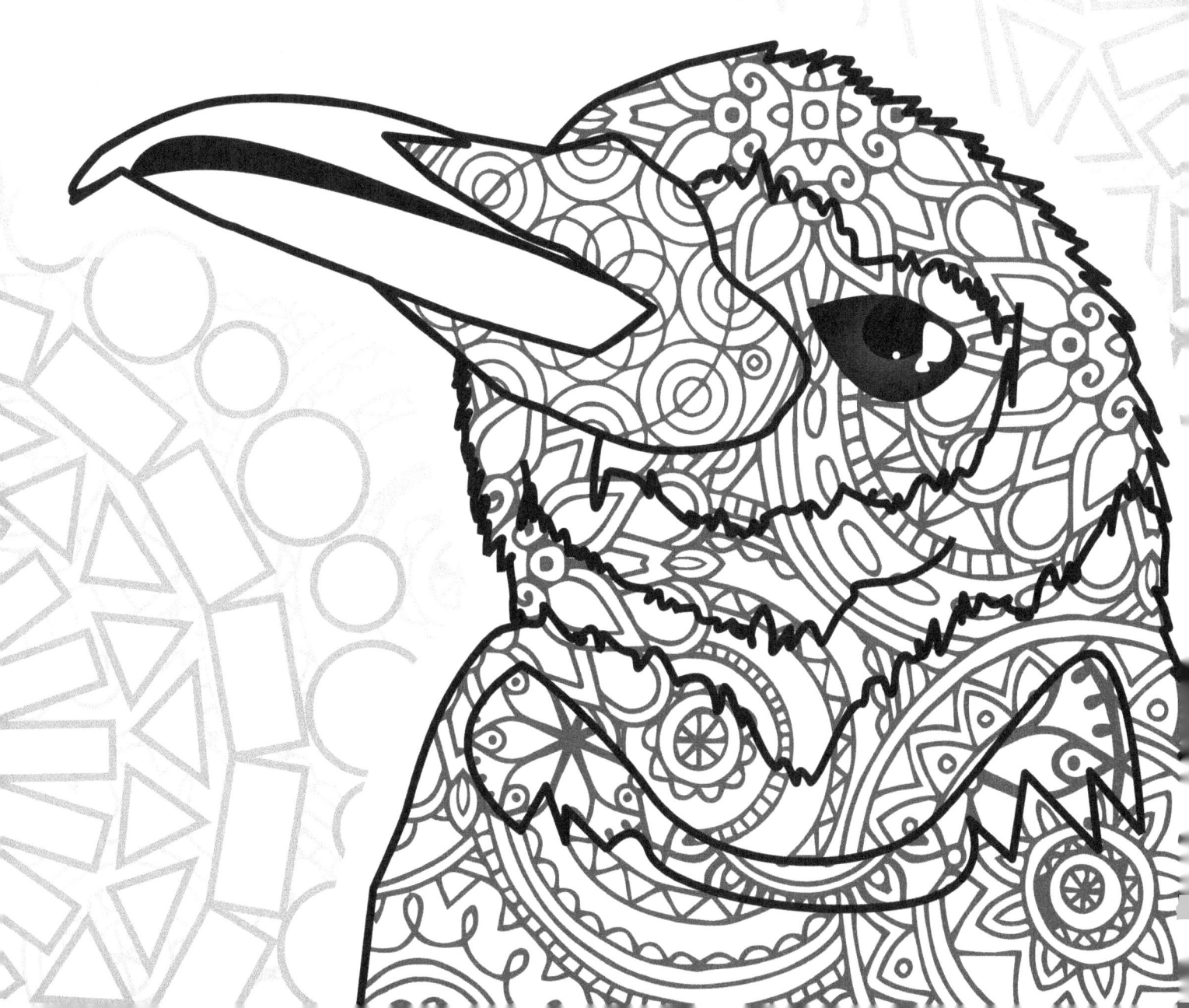

Ready for more?

If you enjoyed this adventure, fasten your seat belts that more are to come! Find me as Emma Russo to keep doing creative Mindfulness in a different way while we enjoy the process.

It would be great if you leave me a review, so many more will benefit from the wisdom of the animal that they carry inside and surrender to the teachings of the Zen masters.

Now that you've had a taste of the benefits of mindfulness, it's not the time to turn back! Keep practicing and free yourself. You will not be able to start a new chapter of your life if you do not close the previous one.

Cheers

Emma R.

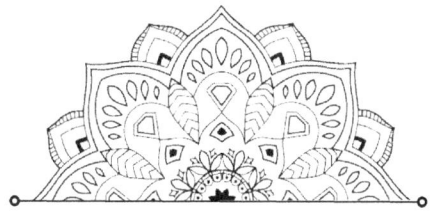